Enriching the Curriculum Through

SERVICE
LEARNING

Edited by Carol W. Kinsley and Kate McPherson

Association for Supervision and Curriculum Development
Alexandria, Virginia

Association for Supervision and Curriculum Development
1250 N. Pitt Street
Alexandria, VA 22314-1453
Telephone (703) 549-9110
FAX (703) 549-3891

ASCD publications present a variety of viewpoints. The views expressed or implied in this book should not be interpreted as official positions of the Association.

Printed in the United States of America.

Gene R. Carter, *Executive Director*
Ronald S. Brandt, *Director of Publications*
Nancy Modrak, *Managing Editor, Books*
Carolyn R. Pool, *Associate Editor*
Biz McMahon, *Assistant Editor*
Gary Bloom, *Manager, Design and Production Services*
Karen Monaco, *Senior Designer*
Stephanie Kenworthy, *Print Production Coordinator*
Valerie Sprague, *Desktop Publisher*

From the Editors:

We welcome readers' comments on ASCD books and other publications. If you would like to give us your opinion of this book or suggest topics for future books, please write to ASCD, Managing Editor of Books, 1250 N. Pitt St., Alexandria, VA 22314.

Price: $15.95
ASCD Stock No.: 1-95057
ISBN: 0-87120-246-8

Library of Congress Cataloging-in-Publication Data

Enriching the curriculum through service learning / edited by Carol W.
    Kinsley and Kate McPherson.
        p.   cm.
    Includes bibliographical references.
    ISBN 0-87120-246-8 (alk. paper)
    1. Student service—United States.   2. Community and school—
United States.   I. Kinsley, Carol W.   II. McPherson, Kate.
III. Association for Supervision and Curriculum Development.
LB220.5.E67   1995
361.3'7—dc20   95-13949
                                                                    CIP

Enriching the Curriculum Through Service Learning

Foreword vii
  Richard W. Riley, Secretary, U.S. Department of Education

Introduction: Changing Perceptions to Integrate Service
Learning in Education 1
  Carol W. Kinsley, Director, Community Service Learning
  Center, Springfield, Massachusetts
  Kate McPherson, Director, Project Service Leadership,
  Vancouver, Washington

Part I. Community Service Learning as a Vehicle for Active Learning

1. Literature in Language Arts: Quilting Lessons in the School
   Curriculum 13
     Jo-Anne Wilson Keenan, School/Family Curriculum
     Integration Teacher, Springfield Public Schools,
     Springfield, Massachusetts

2. Inclusion and Community Service Learning: A Partnership 17
     Mary Chamberlain, Teacher, Rebecca Johnson School,
     Springfield, Massachusetts

3. Social Studies Moves into the Community 21
     Sally Fellows, Teacher, Active Citizenship Today, Omaha,
     Nebraska

4. The Need to Consider Service Learning in Developing
   Future Vocational Education Programs 24
     Harry Silcox, Director, Pennsylvania Institute for
     Environment and Community Service Learning,
     Philadelphia

Part II. Changing the Culture of the School Through Service Learning

5. Community Service Learning Is a Foregone Conclusion at
   the Lincoln Elementary School 31
     Michelle Boorstein, Reporter, Associated Press, Providence,
     Rhode Island

6. Creating a School and Community Culture to Sustain
   Service Learning 36
   *Caroline Allam, Managing Director, KIDS Consortium,
   Portland, Maine*

7. How Do We Make a Difference in Our School and
   Community? 43
   *Len Solo, Principal, Graham & Parks Alternative School,
   Cambridge, Massachusetts*

8. High School: Service Learning and a Caring School
   Community 53
   *Janice M. Reeder, Principal, Gig Harbor High School, Gig
   Harbor, Washington*

9. Service Learning Honors Cultural Diversity 59
   *Wokie Roberts-Weah, Director of National Programs,
   National Youth Leadership Council, St, Paul, Minnesota*

Part III. Service Experiences Encourage Teachers to Facilitate Learning

10. Middle School: Intergenerational Experiences Support
    Teaching and Learning 65
    *Lisa Laplante, Project Manager, Community Service
    Learning Center, Springfield, Massachusetts*

11. Enhancing Peer Mediation Through Community Service
    Learning 69
    *Denise Messina, Teacher, Forest Park Middle School,
    Springfield, Massachusetts*

12. Students Take the Lead in AIDS Education 75
    *Julie Coar, Student, Gig Harbor High School, Gig Harbor,
    Washington*

Part IV. The School as Community Partner

13. Vision for the 21st Century: Seamless Relationship Between
    School and Community 81
    *Peter J. Negroni, Superintendent, Springfield Public
    Schools, Springfield, Massachusetts*

14. Schools and Business Benefit Mutually Through Service
    Learning 85
    *Mike Bookey, President, Digital Network Architects, DNA
    Associates, Inc., Issaquah, Washington*

15. Schools and Community-Based Organizations:
    Partnerships Based on History 89
    Rick Jackson, Vice President, YMCA of Greater Seattle,
    Seattle, Washington

16. Youth Corps Makes Middle School Connection 91
    Ira Harkavy, Director, Center for Community Partnerships,
    University of Pennsylvania, Philadelphia; Cory
    Bowman, Assistant Director, Penn Program for Public
    Service, University of Pennsylvania, Philadelphia

Part V. Reflection

17. Reflection as a Tool for Turning Service Experiences into
    Learning Experiences 99
    Pamela and James Toole, Co-Directors, Compass Institute,
    St. Paul, Minnesota

Conclusion: Challenges for the Future 115
    Kate McPherson and Carol W. Kinsley

Part VI. Service-Learning Resources

Community Service Learning Centers 119

National Organizations 119

Resource Books and Other Materials 120

The *Service Learning Planning and Resource*
    Guide: A Description 124
    Barbara Gomez, Service-Learning Project, Council of Chief
    State School Officers, Washington, D.C.

Standards of Quality for School-Based Service Learning 126
    Alliance for Service Learning in Educational Reform

Seasons of Service 135
    Corporation for National and Community Service

About the Authors 138

Foreword

It is with pleasure that I introduce this timely publication on service learning that will help educators in their efforts to reform schools and improve education. As a response to our national need to reconnect children, families, and schools, service learning can improve learning and instill an ethic of service and citizenship in our youth. Service learning also helps us in our efforts to achieve the National Education Goals.

Advocates of service learning and proponents of school reform are natural allies who share an understanding about what is important to the development of a strong education. Though the two movements developed independently, their goals have converged; and they may now join forces in a common effort to improve education.

People in both movements agree that all children learn more and can provide greater service to society if we challenge them to do more, have higher expectations for them, and hold them to higher learning standards with enriched course content. Both groups know that we can significantly improve students' education through active learning of subject matter in real-life settings. Both groups strive to build on student strengths and interests for learning in the classroom and for service in the community, and they work to make full use of the community and caring adults as learning resources.

All these attributes play an important role in helping us reach the National Education Goals. First, service learning provides an education in good citizenship. By engaging youth in learning activities designed to meet real community needs, we can help students develop an ethic of service, along with the character and habits of community participation needed to ensure that they are prepared for responsible citizenship.

Second, by involving students in hands-on learning, problem solving, and applications of academic knowledge in real settings, service learning can increase students' academic achievement in challenging subjects. When we enrich students' experiences with service activities that enable them to make valued contributions to the community, we can also create a sense of engagement that enhances a student's motivation to complete school.

This sense of engagement and responsibility will continue after formal learning has ended, helping to create a responsible and skilled work force that can participate successfully in a world-class economy and in the democratic life of our nation. When service learning brings youth and adults together in collaborative teams working to solve real problems, students gain personal insight into the knowledge and skills needed to achieve concrete results in the community. For the majority of students who do not enter college directly after high school, service learning also provides valuable career exploration and strategies for entering the work force. And for students too young to be salaried employees, service learning provides a valuable early structured work experience.

Third, service learning contributes to the development of safe schools. By engaging young people in constructive and rewarding in-school and after-school activities, service learning helps keep children involved, productive, and off the street, so they are away from harm's way. And it allows young people and adults to work together to address important community problems, thereby helping to mend the growing sense of disconnection that so many young people feel today. Training students in peer mediation and conflict resolution can also make a significant contribution to our efforts to achieve a disciplined learning environment.

In the United States, we have a pressing need to reconnect our families with their schools, and our schools with their communities. We must reinvent a sense of community if we want our schools to achieve their full potential, bringing together adults, children, teachers, and other members of the community in an effort to improve student learning, responsibility, and citizenship. We know that schools do well when they make new connections—when they involve the business community, the arts and science communities, the university community, and other social services in a common effort to raise standards. Service-learning projects provide the structure needed to engage parents and other adults in our children's education.

Service learning is effective when it is structured to respond to both the needs of the community and the learning needs of students. The service experience must be integrated into the academic program by knowledgeable teachers working with a well-designed curriculum. This book on service learning provides the nation's teaching force with access to information for the continued improvement of the professional skills and knowledge needed to instruct and prepare students to be knowledgeable and productive citizens.

Richard W. Riley
Secretary, U.S. Department of Education

Introduction: Changing Perceptions to Integrate Community Service Learning into Education

Carol Kinsley, Director, Community Service Learning Center,
Springfield, Massachusetts

Kate McPherson, Director, Project Service Leadership,
Vancouver, Washington

Service learning is a powerful educational experience where interest collides with information, values are formed, and action emerges. The learning part has two dimensions: an inner dimension; learning about yourself, your motivation, your values, and an outer dimension; learning about the world, its ways and the underlying cause of the problems that service work addresses (Sawyer 1991).

Community service learning has captured the imagination and gained the support of thousands of teachers across the United States. It began as a way to provide young people with a sense of civic and social responsibility and support them in their growth and development. It has mushroomed into a process and methodology that helps connect young people to their communities and inspires teachers to bring school-reform initiatives to life. As a result, teachers are dramatically changing the dynamic of learning—from static to participatory—by tapping the energy and talent of youth.

The notion of integrating service experiences into curriculum and connecting schools with agencies and neighborhoods has spread from teachers to schools, to community agencies, and to entire communities. Service-learning experiences connect students to their communities, enrich students' learning, and help them develop personally, socially and academically. People in these communities believe that in performing service, youth learn to understand the meaning of community beyond self and develop a sense of responsibility and respect for others.

• In Tumwater, Washington, civics students helped new immigrants pass their citizenship tests.

• Industrial design students in Tacoma, Washington, built a wheelchair for an 18-month-old child with multiple sclerosis.

• Elementary students at Stocking Elementary School in Grand Rapids, Michigan, and Chestnut Middle School in Springfield, Massachusetts, wrote and illustrated stories that they gave to new mothers to encourage them to read to their children.

• Middle school students in Agawam, Massachusetts, and in many other communities are learning about history through interaction with elderly partners.

• Students at Putnam Vocational Technical High School in Springfield, Massachusetts, are creating a health center to serve students' health needs.

• In Issaquah, Washington, high school students are designing a districtwide technology network, providing technology training for teachers and managing a communitywide e-mail network.

To illustrate both the promise and the practice of service learning, this book focuses on the stories and examples of practitioners. Rather than describing the research and practice theoretically, we asked people from many different schools and locations to reflect on and share their service-learning stories to illustrate how they tap service learning to bring life to learning. This format resists being a tightly knit volume— instead, it captures the rich tapestry of service learning through the experiences described by administrators, teachers, university faculty, and students.

Roots of Service

A tradition of community service goes back to early U.S. history. In 1830, Alexis de Tocqueville first recorded this unique phenomenon in *Democracy in America*. As he observed the civic and social support citizens gave to their young nation, he called these acts "habits of the heart" (Bellah, Madsen, Sullivan, Swidler, and Tipton 1986, Preface, p. vii). He saw these "habits" as a counterpoint to the individualism represented in the society and as a way to unify the political community and "thus ultimately support the maintenance of free institutions." The term "habits of the heart" has been revived in the past decade to help refocus our thinking and to remind us that a fundamental and natural part of democracy is based on people helping and caring for one another. Building on this theme, Langton and Miller (1988) observe that the "principle of commitment to others is the counterpoint of America's emphasis on individualism, and both constitute the basic underpinnings of our society" (p. 25).

Historically, community service has been part of the activities of families, churches, community organizations such as the Girl and Boy Scouts, and school groups including Key Clubs and National Honor Societies.

In the early 1980s, many educational and political leaders began to advocate for increased involvement of youth in community service activities, citing the need for youth not only to understand their rights as individuals but their responsibilities toward each other (Neal 1986). In addition, advocates saw the need in education to break the isolation, the emphasis on self, and the lack of connections between youth and their communities (Boyer 1987a). David Hornbeck (1989) blamed the crisis in our society and in education not on lower math and science scores, but on the fact that we care too little for one another and too much for ourselves. These leaders have begun to view community service as a vehicle for youth development, the advancement of school reform, and, ultimately, community renewal.

In addition to the traditional emphasis on community service, service learning has other roots, as follows.

Service is consciously transformed into service learning. The transition from traditional community service to service learning occurs "when there is a deliberate connection made between service and learning opportunities which are then accompanied by conscious and thoughtfully designed occasions for reflecting on the service experience" (Alliance for Service Learning in Education Reform 1993; see "Standards of Quality for School-Based Service Learning," by the Alliance, in the "Resources" section of this book). The added dimension of learning provides depth to young people's experiences, helps support their social and personal development, and provides integrated curriculum and instruction to support school reform experiences.

Service learning has roots in citizenship education. One important function of schools is to prepare students to become contributing citizens to their classroom, school or community. Service learning is a valuable strategy to achieve this goal because

- it encourages youth to understand the way their community is governed and how to have input and impact.
- when students actively participate in their community, they see that they *can make a difference* and will, we hope, make participation a habit.
- it develops the capacity to see issues from a broader perspective.
- it enables students to see the relationship between their private rights and interests and those of the public good.
- community involvement develops the "habits of the heart" and fosters an ethic of service and volunteerism without which our communities could not survive.
- as students extend themselves to help others, they feel a greater sense of social responsibility.

Service learning has roots in experiential education. The educational philosophy of John Dewey, Ralph Tyler, and Hilda Taba stressed the importance of integrating learning experiences into the curriculum to provide a framework for learning. These educators, as well as Piaget, Coleman, and Kolb, have long urged teachers to teach through experiences. Dewey (cited in Davis, Maher, and Noddings 1990) maintained: "The mind is not individual but social, and learning is a by-product of social activities." Dewey believed that all curriculum must be generated out of social situations based on organized principles but founded on the twin pillars of the capacity of the child and the demands of the environment.

Tyler (1949) maintained that learning occurs "through the active behavior of the student; it is what he does that he learns, not what the teacher does" (p. 63).

Taba (1962) provided an in-depth approach to the process of curriculum development. Her analysis and descriptions of content organization and design provide concrete ways to produce curriculum that will actively engage students in learning. Some service-learning practitioners are guided by her process, through which teachers develop the objectives of education, integrate learning experiences, and develop teaching-learning units. She urged educators to use the concerns of the learners to increase motivation and connect the essential elements of education.

A contemporary variation on this theme is "constructivist theory," which suggests that "people are not recorders of information, but builders of knowledge structures" (Resnick and Klopfer 1989, p. 4). Constructivism, as identified by Davis and colleagues (cited in Peterson and Knapp 1993), concerns the redefinition of the teacher's role, away from *directing* and *telling* toward "guiding student activity, modeling behavior, and providing the examples and counter-examples" (p. 144).

Service learning has roots in youth development. Service has long been viewed as a powerful way to develop character, foster an ethic of service, and nurture a sense of membership in the community. In the agrarian culture of the 19th century, youth were essential for the survival of the family and the society. They naturally developed a sense of personal value and an understanding of their role in the community as they provided for the family, cared for animals, and planted and harvested crops.

As our society moved from agrarian to urban, the journey from youth to adulthood has not developed appropriate ways for youth to gain a sense of purpose and become connected to their communities. As Harold Howe states, "We have no use in our economic system for young people between the ages of twelve and eighteen, and precious little use in our community affairs. So we suggest you sit quietly, behave yourselves, and study hard in the schools we provide as a holding pen until we are ready to accept you into the adult world" (Howe, quoted in Boyer 1987b, p. 7).

Many schools, in an attempt to address Howe's concern with self-esteem curriculum, direct students to talk about self-esteem and do fabricated activities. Service-learning advocates suggest, however, that opportunities to make real contributions to their school and community will better nurture the self-esteem of young people and give them a positive sense of self.

Conrad and Hedin (1989), based on 20 years of teaching community service in the classroom and a review of research in the field, hypothesized that well-designed community service programs would have a positive effect on youth in the following areas:

Personal Growth and Development

- Self-esteem
- Personal efficacy (sense of worth and competence)
- Ego and moral development
- Exploration of new roles, identities, and interests
- Willingness to take risks, accept new challenges
- Revised and reinforced values and beliefs
- Taking responsibility for, accepting consequences of own actions

Intellectual Development and Academic Learning

- Basic academic skills (expressing ideas, reading, calculating)

- Higher-level thinking skills (open-mindedness, problem solving, critical thinking)
- Content and skills directly related to service experiences
- Skills in learning from experience (to observe, ask questions, apply knowledge)
- Motivation to learn and retention of knowledge
- Insight, judgment, understanding—the nuances that can't be explained in a book or lecture but are often the most important things of all to know

Social Growth and Development

- Social responsibility, concern for the welfare of others
- Political efficacy
- Civic participation
- Knowledge and exploration of service-related careers
- Understanding and appreciation of, and ability to relate to, people from a wider range of backgrounds and life situations

Conrad and Hedin (1989) recognize that service learning and its outcomes are difficult to evaluate because service learning is not a "definable activity like taking notes at a lecture" (p. 20). Students participate in many types of activities and experience them in different ways. Further, it is difficult to measure growth and development; many different factors, including the effect of the service experience, can come into play. Fortunately, researchers are attempting to quantify the effect of service learning on youth development

For example, in a case study conducted on the integration of community service learning into the curriculum of a middle school in Springfield, Massachusetts, teachers and students reported that the service experiences added to the students' academic, social, and personal development (Kinsley 1992). The learning situations included involvement in active and cooperative learning, problem solving, and multicultural experiences. As a result, Kinsley reported, middle school students began to see their classroom and school as a community and made connections to the larger community, as well. Their service-learning activities included the following:

- Advocating to the local School Committee for action on an environmental issue based on the research they had conducted
- Providing ushers for a local puppet theater on a regular basis
- Learning the writing process together with elders in the senior citizens' residence next door
- Conducting after-school service at a nearby social service center

Not only did students' experiences enhance their understanding of basic skills and help them apply content information, but the different vehicles helped them understand the meaning of community, the benefits of reaching out and sharing with others, and the concept of giving their time without thought of reward.

Teachers observed that as students learned more about the community, they gained a stronger sense of themselves. In addition, the service experiences helped students break down stereotypes and barriers as they interacted with elderly people, various ethnic and racial groups, and adults from the various service sites. Manners and respect increased as the students successfully participated in their service activities (Kinsley 1992).

A 1993 study in the Springfield Public Schools suggested that service learning is a powerful motivator for learning. Two control groups were surveyed to determine the effect of community service learning on learning. Of the students surveyed, 90.5 percent responded that they enjoyed learning their topic when community service learning was part of their work, in contrast to 67.2 percent of the group not participating in service learning.

Educators and citizens alike recognize that our youth need support. We often hear the African proverb, "It takes a village to raise a child." Service learning provides a way to make connections with the "village" and provide youth with the support they need as they discover who they are and how they can become part of their communities.

Service learning has roots in school reform. Seymour Sarason, in *The Predictable Failure of School Reform* (1991), states that true school reform cannot be accomplished without a change in the traditional authoritarian classroom. Although this change is difficult, many communities are making significant efforts to restructure and improve school programs.

These efforts often mirror the community service-learning process:

- Schools attempt to replace rote learning with authentic learning, using activities that enable students to apply content information and skills to complex and real situations.
- Teachers become facilitators of learning, assisting students as they gather, examine, and synthesize information, then draw conclusions in problem-solving activities.
- Teachers reach out to the community to make new partnerships and provide real-life experiences for students.

- Youth contribute to the learning process as they become teachers/mentors. Through this work, they develop the ability to analyze abstract material and place it in a meaningful framework to understand what is needed.
- Schools move outside their traditional boundaries by extending learning beyond the school building to create more vital learning communities.
- As teachers and youth link the knowledge and information to their school or community in meaningful ways and youth realize that they can "make a difference," they all find service learning a powerful way to teach and learn.

As educators work toward school reform, they are discovering that multiple interventions are essential for significant school change: collaborative strategies, the development of new and old basic skills, new roles for students, integrated curriculum, authentic assessment, infusion of technology, new linkages with the community, and a restructuring of time. Service learning, by its very nature, has proven to be a powerful connector for these frequently disparate interventions. And service learning provides a vehicle to complement and implement reform initiatives such as cooperative learning, active learning, thematic units, and authentic learning.

Although service learning is not the sole answer for school restructuring, many teachers, students, and administrators are realizing its value in revitalizing learning, regenerating the school and community, and providing a powerful way for our young people to develop self-esteem and social responsibility. Service learning also provides a way for teachers to give meaning to learning while motivating students and for the school as a whole to unify its often-fragmented school reform efforts.

The information in this book illustrates the many ways in which educators, students, and community members are bringing together the various aspects of school reform. Practitioners from many schools and communities share thoughtful service-learning programs that alter the way teachers teach, the way the school day operates, the ways young people learn and grow in the context of their schooling, the way young people can connect to and help build their community, and the way school is viewed in the community.

References

Alliance for Service Learning in Education Reform. (1993). *Standards of Quality and Excellence for School-Based Service Learning*. Washington, D.C.: Council of Chief State School Officers.

Bellah, R.N., R. Madsen, W.M. Sullivan, A. Swidler, and S.M. Tipton. (1986). *Habits of the Heart: Individualism and Commitment in American Life*. New York: Harper & Row.

Boyer, E. (1987a). "Foreword." In *Student Service*, edited by C. Harrison. Princeton: Carnegie Foundation for the Advancement of Teaching.

Boyer, E.L. (October 1987b). "Service Linking School to Life." *Community Education Journal*, p. 7.

Conrad, D., and D. Hedin. (December 1989). *High School Community Service: A Review of Research and Programs*. Washington, D.C.: National Center on Effective Secondary Schools, U.S. Department of Education, Office of Educatonal Research and Improvement; and Madison: Wisconsin Center for Education Research, School of Education, University of Wisconsin-Madison.

Hornbeck, D. (November 13, 1989). Speech presented at the Growing Hope Conference, National Youth Leadership Council, St. Paul, Minnesota.

Kinsley, C. (1992). "A Case Study: The Integration of Community Service Learning into the Curriculum by an Interdisciplinary Team of Teachers at an Urban Middle School." Doctoral diss., University of Massachusetts.

Langton, S., and F. Miller. (Spring 1988). "Youth Community Service." *Equity & Choice* 4, 3: 25–33.

Neal, R. (1986). Speech presented at Youth Service Recognition Day, Springfield Public Schools, Springfield, Massachusetts.

Peterson, P.L., and N.F. Knapp. (1993). "Inventing and Reinventing Ideas: "Constructivist Teaching and Learning in Mathematics." In *Challenges and Achievements of American Education*, ASCD 1993 Yearbook, edited by G. Cawelti. Alexandria, Va.: ASCD.

Resnick, L.B., and C.E. Klopfer. (1989). *Toward the Thinking Curriculum: Current Cognitive Research*. Alexandria, Va.: ASCD.

Sarason, S. (1990). *The Predictable Failure of School Reform*. San Francisco: Jossey-Bass.

Sawyer, D. (October 1991). Speech presented at the Wingspread Conference, Racine, Wisconsin.

Taba, H. (1962). *Curriculum Development Theory and Practice*. New York: San Francisco Press.

Tyler, R. (1949). *Basic Principles of Curriculum*. Chicago: The University of Chicago Press.

Part I

Community Service Learning as a Vehicle for Active Learning

1

Literature in Language Arts: Quilting Lessons in the School Curriculum

Jo-Anne Wilson Keenan, School/Family Curriculum Integration Teacher, Springfield Public Schools, Springfield, Massachusetts

Just as heirloom quilts grow from tiny scraps of fabric, so several opportunities for community service learning grew from a patchwork of stories read in my combined 1st and 2nd grade classroom.

Learning experiences in our multicultural urban classroom evolved through thematic studies. Children's literature lies at the heart of these experiences and was a primary means through which the children made connections to the world outside. As part of our studies, each student's family was invited into the classroom to share their special talents. The family visits became a form of community service to our classroom.

The first conversation about quilts in our classroom resulted from my reading *The Patchwork Quilt*, by Valerie Flournoy (1985), to the class. The book was a logical choice for adding a warm touch to our study of families and communities. It tells of a girl and her family who

---

The events in this chapter took place when I was teaching in a multi-age 1st and 2nd grade classroom at the Mary O. Pottenger School, a public school in Springfield, Massachusetts. This school serves children from ethnically, racially, and socioeconomically diverse communities within Springfield. A significant proportion of the children are bused from distant neighborhoods to achieve racial balance. The school serves a substantial number of low-income families. In the year that the quilting lessons took place, the school's population of approximately 510 children, K–5, was about 51 percent Puerto Rican, 21 percent African American, 26 percent European American, and 2 percent Asian.

13

work together to complete a quilt for their grandmother after she is taken ill and is unable to complete it by herself.

When I planned to read the story to the children, I had not anticipated the enthusiastic personal connections that they would make to the story. As I read, the children noticed the quilts in the story and said, "That's the quilt I have!" and "That's a quilt like mine!" The children also remarked that their grandmothers had pincushions like the one in the story. The quilt stuffing, they thought, would make the quilt soft and comfortable.

The reaction to the first story was so positive that we sought out other stories about quilts and began reading and exploring them together. As we read, we discovered ways in which quilt stories teach lessons about how people work together and serve each other in their families and communities.

In *Sam Johnson and the Blue Ribbon Quilt*, by Lisa Ernst (1983), a group of men compete against a group of women to win a blue ribbon in the quilting contest at the county fair. In the end, when both quilts are nearly ruined, everyone learns the value of working together. As we read this book, we noted the quilt patterns that form the borders of the pages and talked about how the name of each of each pattern fit the design. But more important, we noted the value of cooperation among members of a community.

We also read *The Quilt Story*, by Tony Johnston (1985), and discussed the way in which quilts preserve the history of a family as they are passed down from one generation to the next. As the days passed, we continued to collect and read other stories about quilts. The children and I brought in quilts from home and hung them in the classroom. The children chose one to sit on during their workshop time. We were completely immersed in quilts and their stories when one student, Hector, announced that his mother would come into school and make a quilt for the class.

On the day that Hector's mother came to sew the quilt, her husband, daughter, son, and grandson all came with her. They helped her carry the sewing machine and fabric. They were all dressed in outfits that she had made for them. As she sewed, the children told the family members about the stories we had read. Hector's dad said that sewing was not just for women. The children agreed, and ran to show him the copy of *Sam Johnson and the Blue Ribbon Quilt*. Hector's mother spoke mostly Spanish, so one child took up the task of asking her questions for those of us who did not speak Spanish fluently. This child performed a service for the community by helping everyone participate in the conversation. When the quilt was finished, we all sat in a circle and passed it around so everyone could take a firsthand look and thank Hector's mother. One child said, "It's so beautiful, and it's snugly."

Another boy added, "My great-great-grandma gave her daughter a quilt, and her daughter gave her daughter a quilt, and she gave it to me!"

By the time the meeting was over, we had declared that Hector's mother's quilt would be our classroom quilt. From now on, we would pass it around during "peace meetings" in our classroom. During these meetings, we brainstormed solutions to conflicts within our classroom community. The quilt now became a symbol of harmony within the classroom. We also decided that when a new school year came and the 2nd graders moved on to a new classroom, the quilt would remain in our room. It would be passed down to the next class, just as our classmate's quilt had been passed down.

When the new school year arrived, the children moved on—but the quilt stayed. One morning in the beginning of September, Hector came back to the room holding a beautiful, blue crib-sized quilt. The student council was going to sponsor a quilting bee as a community-service-learning project. Children and parents would make quilts for babies with AIDS who were being cared for at a Springfield medical center. Hector and his mother did not wait for the quilting bee, but had carried the lessons from the quilt stories into a service for our entire Springfield community.

Bibliography

Ernst, L.C. (1983). *Sam Johnson and the Blue Ribbon Quilt*. New York: Lorthrop, Lee and Shepard.

Flournoy, V. (1985). *The Patchwork Quilt*. New York: Dial Books.

Johnston, T. (1985). *The Quilt Story*. New York: Putnam.

For more information about peace meetings, see:

Hopkins, S., & J. Winters, eds. (1990). *Discover the World: Empowering Children to Value Themselves, Others and the Earth*. Philadelphia: New Society Publishers.

Other favorite stories featuring quilts:

Hopkins, D. (1993). *Sweet Clara and the Freedom Quilt*. New York: Alfred A. Knopf.

Kinsey-Warnock, N. (1989). *The Canadian Geese Quilt*. New York: Dell Publishing.

Mitchell, M.K. (1993). *Uncle Jed's Barber Shop*. New York: Simon and Schuster.

Polacco, P. (1988). *The Keeping Quilt*. New York: Simon and Schuster.

Ringold, F. (1991). *Tar Beach*. New York: Scholastic.

Acknowledgments

The family visits described in this chapter were done in collaboration with Judith Solsken, of the Reading and Writing Program, and Jerri Willett, of the Cultural Diversity and Curriculum Reform Program, of the University of Massachusetts at Amherst. Research on this project was funded during 1991–92 by a grant from the National Council of Teachers of English.

2

Inclusion and Community Service Learning: A Partnership

Mary Chamberlain, Teacher, Rebecca Johnson School,
Springfield, Massachusetts

Teachers and students, already burdened by seemingly overwhelming curriculum demands, are seeing more areas of study moved into the schools as a result of today's societal needs. Community service learning must not be perceived as yet another burden, but as an integrated part of the curriculum, an enhancement to teaching and learning.

I began to weave community service learning into the 6th grade English curriculum in 1991–93, following the recommendations of middle school task forces (Atwell 1987). During this time, inclusion—the integration of special education and bilingual students with regular students—became part of the Springfield Public Schools education program. The following is the story of the development of a community service learning/inclusion partnership, the integration of community service learning into the curriculum, and real writing for real purposes.

Rebecca Johnson School, a K–8 magnet school of about 900 students, is an inner-city school with a diverse population of students, some of whom are bused to school.

Kennedy Middle School, the partnership school, has a population of approximately 650 students. In this urban setting, many students are bused from all sections of the city, and some students who live in the neighborhood walk. There is an ethnically diverse group of Afro-American, Hispanic, and white students. This public middle school is situated in a community that has a range of middle to low economic levels.

Developing a Partnership

Beginning in 1991, my 6th grade Language Arts classes created a partnership with two Developmental Skills classes at Kennedy Middle School. Children in these classes have severe mental and physical disabilities, such as cerebral palsy, hearing and sight loss, seizure disorders, and limited or no verbal skills. During the first year, 6th graders visited the Developmental Skills classes twice a week on a rotating basis. With the help of an Inclusion Grant, the second year's partnership shifted from reverse mainstreaming to an inclusive model, bringing the Developmental Skills students into the 6th graders' classroom. While ten or twelve 6th graders worked with five to six special education students, the rest of the class worked in cooperative poetry groups. Each week the 6th grade partners rotated to work with the special education students.

Sixth graders kept a Community Service Learning Log in which they reflected on their experience. In the second year, 6th graders also partnered with 8th graders as they wrote, directed, and produced two Dr. Seuss plays. The troupe performed their plays at the local Shriners' Hospital for Crippled Children as a vehicle for expanding their work with children with disabilities to the larger community.

Was the second year's partnership to be called inclusion or community service learning? Community service learning is exactly what its name implies. It is a service performed to help the community. It isn't new. Consciously adding a learning component to community service *is* new. An important part of the learning component is reflection, when teachers allow time for students to think back on their service through discussions, writing, drawing, and other media. Then, teachers hope, students integrate the learning into their lives to help them become active and responsible citizens.

Inclusion is more a state of mind or a philosophy than a methodology. It's the belief that all children can learn in some capacity, and that all children, despite disabilities or ethnicity, can be integrated into one environment and learn from each other (Kate Fenton, Inclusion Specialist, Springfield, Mass., personal communication, 1994)

As students began the second year of the partnership and reflected on their experiences, I would often say to them that I was confused. I didn't know if the partnership was community service learning or inclusion. It was a pilot program in which special education students were being included in a regular education classroom. Yet regular education students were providing a service to their school community through the partnership. By combining the two processes, each reinforced the other. Inclusion activities provided the vehicle for student interaction, and the community-service-learning process called for students' conscious reflection on their experiences working together.

The Partnership and the Curriculum

Did this partnership interfere with the English curriculum? Not at all. Based on the theory of writing process, the curriculum requires students to learn the techniques and strategies of a writing workshop. Writing can be integrated through literature or writing units.

When my students began the partnership with the Developmental Skills classes, the experience gave them a basis for real writing for real purposes. They had a ready-made topic: their feelings and learning experiences resulting from their work with the students in the Developmental Skills classes.

Free writing was a common reflective activity. After a class discussion, they would free-write for 10–15 minutes, using these questions as guides: What did you do? How did you feel? and What did you learn? As a culminating activity, they prepared a report for the Exceptional People's Awareness Day organized by Kennedy Middle School's Special Education Department. In preparing this report, they followed the "writing workshop" steps, as follows:

> After a class discussion (prewriting), the students decided they wanted to present their report as a picture book (prewriting). They outlined and organized the sequence of the picture book and chose what page they wanted to work on (prewriting). They wrote about the beginning of the program. The middle of the book included descriptive paragraphs of each Developmental Skills student. The conclusion was a list of what they learned through reflection on community service (drafting). As the students reworked their pages, they decided to include a dedication page and a page about the authors (revision). They then edited their work, and I published their book on the computer (editing and publication).

The students were actively involved in this writing project. They knew that they were experts because their writing was based on their own community-service-learning experiences. Because they made decisions on presentation and content, they owned the writing. And because I was comfortable with the knowledge that students were experimenting with many writing strategies, techniques, and styles and integrating them into their experiences as writers, I was able to give them plenty of time. The three basics of writing—time, ownership, and response—were an integral part of this report (see Atwell 1987).

Real Purposes

The class was an active workshop. Students constantly responded because they had a real audience—the people attending the Exceptional People's Awareness Day Exhibit.

The genre chosen by the students, the picture book, incorporating all aspects of the writing process, supported the curriculum. Real writing for real purposes supported the regular education students. And the community service learning/inclusion process supported the special education students. Because there was such a fine line between community service learning and inclusion, the two processes supported and reinforced each other. This fine line enabled us to weave curriculum into real-life experiences and enrich the learning of both regular and special education students.

Reference

Atwell, N. (1987). *In the Middle*. Portsmouth, N.H.: Heinemann.

3

Social Studies Moves into the Community

Sally Fellows, Teacher, Active Citizenship Today,
Omaha, Nebraska

Active Citizenship Today, a program of service-learning pilot projects in the Omaha Public Schools, demonstrates service learning with a corollary, the examination of public policy. Five projects, involving students in geography, history, and government classes, illustrate what students have learned through community service.

From Omaha to Washington, D.C.

One project, developed by a high school Honors Geography class, began by asking students what they wanted the United States to look like in 10 years and what needed to be done to achieve that goal. They isolated what they considered to be the country's most serious problem: the budget deficit. They then invited knowledgeable people to speak to the class on the deficit and potential solutions to the problem. Among the speakers were the mayor of the City of Omaha, the governor of Nebraska, and the congressman from Nebraska's Second District. After the class felt they had acquired as much information as possible, they developed a series of recommendations and then surveyed other social studies classes, families, and neighbors on their reactions to the recommendations. Armed with this information, the class developed proposals for how the federal government ought to deal with the budget deficit.

Two representatives of the class went to Washington, D.C., and presented the report to a member of President Clinton's staff and requested that it be forwarded to the President. They later received acknowledgment of the report from the President's Office. Although the students realized that the budget deficit was not the sort of problem they could solve themselves, they wanted to have some input on an issue so crucial to their future.

State Expert Witnesses

A high school government class examined the bills introduced in the Nebraska legislature for a year and decided to concentrate on one that proposed lowering the blood alcohol level for the definition of "drunk driving." The students invited an emergency room nurse, a drug and alcohol counselor, and a policeman to talk with them about the bill. The class traveled to the state capitol where they met with several state senators, including one who had co-introduced the bill. Students formulated their opinions on the bill and, as a final step, wrote letters to their senators. Unfortunately, the bill died in committee. This was another lesson: one in the reality of politics.

Community History and Geography

A geography class decided to combine a community-needs survey and a lesson in geography. The teacher presented background about the community, and the class gathered information about the history of Omaha from local museums. The head of the Historical Preservation Section of the City Planning Office took the students on a bus tour of the neighborhood, pointing out different types of domestic architecture. The students then began their own survey, recording every single building in eight blocks of the shopping district and its present use. City directories in the public library helped them determine what kinds of buildings had been on each lot over the past 100 years. Using computers, they made a series of historical maps showing how the types of businesses in the community had changed over the years and discussed the reasons for the changes. They then drew up a community-needs survey based on their research.

Welfare Recommendations

Another government class took note of the fact that the Governor of Nebraska had appointed a task force to make recommendations about changes in the welfare system. They invited two state senators from the task force and the Douglas County Commissioner responsible for oversight of welfare to discuss the welfare system and the suggested improvements. A critique of the task force plan was followed by students' recommendations for welfare system change. Finally, the governor visited the high school to receive the students' report and discuss it with them.

Student Museum

An American History class teamed up with the local Western Heritage Museum to learn about the creation and funding of the museum, the acquisition of artifacts, and the development of exhibits. The class discussed society's need for and support of museums. Working in groups, students chose a topic for an exhibit which they will create. The museum and the school will host a reception for the students and their parents and will display the students' exhibits. The students will serve as junior docents at the museum.

*　　*　　*

These are examples of the way in which projects can be developed around public policy questions. In each project, students incorporate the policy examination of service into their academic studies and make policy recommendations, or provide service relating to the issue in some way. Students are using the community as a laboratory to learn about the world in which they live.

4

The Need to Consider Service Learning in Developing Future Vocational Education Programs

Harry Silcox, Director, Pennsylvania Institute for Service Learning, Philadelphia, Pennsylvania

Most high school vocational education programs are characterized as "school-to-work transition" or "preparation for employment." These programs are under considerable pressure for several reasons: the failure of many schools to place graduates in areas of training, the ever-increasing expense of providing up-to-date equipment for vocational education classes, and employers' negative perceptions of the ability of high school students. Many people working in the field of vocational education see competency-based youth apprenticeship or citizenship education as the solution to the problems inherent in traditional classroom-based vocational education.

In solving these problems, schools must reach out to communities for real-life experiences and to industry for training on modern equipment. Vocational education should prepare students with a business/community-based approach, particularly in view of the current emphasis on outcome-based education, which favors apprenticeship models over classroom models.

Service Learning Defined

Community service programs—where students use the skills they've learned in school to carry out meaningful projects in the community—have become popular, even to the point of being advocated in President Clinton's National Service Act of 1993. Such programs become service-learning programs when teachers blend the service performed into the school curriculum. This community-based program is similar to school transition programs, with the exception that students receive no financial reward as part of community service learning.

For the purpose of identifying the connections between service learning and job preparation, the federal legislative definition of "service learning" contained in the National Service Act of 1993 is most revealing:

> The term *service learning* means a method:
>
> - under which students learn and develop through active participation in thoughtfully organized service experiences that meet actual community needs and that are coordinated in collaboration with the school and community;
>
> - that is integrated into the students' academic curriculum or provides structured time for a student to think, talk, or write about what the student did and saw during the actual service activity;
>
> - that provides students with opportunities to use newly acquired skills and knowledge in real-life situations in their own communities; and
>
> - that enhances what is taught in school by extending student learning beyond the classroom and into the community and helps to foster the development of a sense of caring for others.

It is clear that the methods used in service learning parallel efforts in job training programs. Leaders in both fields are beginning to see the symbiosis between service learning and future employment.

Symbiosis Between Service Learning and Job Training

Hilary Pennington, President of Jobs for the Future, sums up the argument for combining service learning and job training:

We see service learning as a close cousin to work-based learning, one which shares many of its benefits. For example, service learning is one of the few opportunities for students to experience what it means to contribute to society—to make a difference—especially during a period of adolescent growth when this experience is very developmentally important. It re-connects the students to his or her community, and the school (if the effort is school-based) to its neighborhood. Moreover, service learning, like apprenticeship experiences, contextualizes the student's learning, whether that learning stems from the classroom, the workplace, or the service project. Service learning, if done well, provides the environment in which students can gain organizational, team, and problem-posing and -solving skills, and other attitudes and capabilities necessary to future work and learning (quoted by Halperin 1992).

Sam Halperin (1992), of the American Youth Forum, agrees with Pennington. He believes we can better address two issues through service learning: *scale* and *access*. Halperin sees that "apprenticeship" programs face enormous difficulties as they reach for scale. Using well-designed service-learning experiences, we may be able to achieve many of the learning goals of the apprenticeship work experience through placements in both private and public, profit and nonprofit sectors. Though service learning often lacks the formality and content of the paid work experience, it does provide students with a broader spectrum of experience in the community and the workplace.

Student access is particularly important when schools consider the use of service-learning programs to foster preemployment skills and job readiness. Most apprenticeship programs require students to have working papers, meaning that they must be at least 16 years old. This places such programs in the 11th and 12th grades. Unfortunately, a majority of urban, non-college-bound youth who could most profit from such programs have dropped out of school before the 11th grade. The result is that students in most need of such training are the least likely to receive it. The ideal solution to this dilemma is to use service-learning experiences for students younger than 16 to provide job readiness skills in real-life situations.

Stephen F. Hamilton (1990) of Cornell University endorses such a system of service programs. He advocates apprenticeship programs that combine community service programs in what he calls a "comprehensive apprenticeship system." Hamilton argues that apprenticeship programs in countries such as Germany and Denmark fit their culture and have established traditions of skill training accepted by industry. No such circumstances exist in the United States. Rather, he feels, community service learning in action can augment work experience programs to achieve the same training results as in the European countries.

To Hamilton, community service learning gives younger adolescents "worker roles with a degree of complexity and level of responsibility that they could not ordinarily find in paid employment" (1990, p. 154). Moreover, volunteer service projects undertaken by groups of young people provide experiences in planning and management that are unavailable to them in most work settings. By initiating projects that otherwise would not exist, youth take control of the decision-making process from which they are normally excluded in adult settings. In addition, service programs permit student diversity and work-based skill training.

Service Learning in Specific Classes

Beyond the large-scale employment preparation projects, many vocational education teachers promote service learning in their classrooms. In addition, there are some attempts to promote large-scale programs that encourage teachers to try service-learning methodology when developing job-training programs. The Readers' Digest Fund, for example, has given seven schools in New York City over $1 million to combine service learning and preparation for employment (Walks of Life Program). Such service-learning projects use personal and vocational skills learned in the classroom to complete projects in the community. Despite the limited scope of such programs, they do exist and provide working models for the future. For example, a construction class rehabilitates houses for the poor; carpentry classes construct a courtroom in Pittsburgh; electrical classes also help rehabilitate houses. The only limitation for these vocational education service-learning classes is the imagination of the instructors.

The experience of the Pennsylvania Institute for Community Service Learning in training teachers has shown that the group of vocational education teachers most willing to become involved in service learning are home economics teachers. According to Carol Buncie, a teacher at Garden Spot High School in Pennsylvania, home economics is a subject area that has lost large numbers of teachers and students because "teaching home-making skills to females is no longer appropriate in a society that fosters sex equality." Service learning has enabled home economics teachers to stretch the curriculum beyond the traditional home-making mentality. They are excited by the possibilities fostered by intergenerational programs and human service projects that make their subject more than just a training ground for future homemakers.

*   *   *

Clearly, service-learning programs provide the missing link for school-to-work transition at all levels of the educational ladder. If Hamilton, Pennington, and Halperin are right, service learning must become part of programs that accelerate preparation for employment. What impact this movement will have on U.S. education is still unknown. But it offers the most hope and the best opportunity for universal involvement by our schools and communities in meaningful preparation for life.

Bibliography

Halperin, S. (April 1992). "Proposal for Career/Service-Learning Pre-Apprenticeship Program." Unpublished manuscript.

Hamilton, S.F. (1990). *Apprenticeship for Adulthood: Preparing Youth for the Future.* New York: Free Press.

Kennedy, T., and M. Rodale. (1987). *Community Options: The Regeneration Project.* Emmaus, Pa.: Rodale Press.

Youth and America's Future: The William T. Grant Foundation Commission on Work, Family and Citizenship. (1988). *The Forgotten Half: Non-College Youth in America.* Washington, D.C.: Author.

Youth and America's Future: The William T. Grant Foundation Commission on Work, Family and Citizenship. (1988). *The Forgotten Half: Pathways to Success for America's Youth and Young Families.* Washington, D.C.: Author.

Part II

Changing the Culture of Schools Through Service Learning

5

Community Service Learning Is a Foregone Conclusion at the Lincoln Elementary School

Michelle Boorstein, Reporter,
Associated Press, Providence, Rhode Island

For the staff at Lincoln Elementary School in Springfield, Massachusetts, articulating the many ways in which community service learning affects their school is nearly impossible. The principal says he doesn't require people to do community service. Yet, on any given day, students all over the school are learning through service projects.

"Community service is just something that we do; you don't say to someone, 'Go do a community service project,'" said Enrique Figueredo, Lincoln's principal for the past three years and an avid proponent of community service learning. "It is part of our school. We live it," he said.

Lincoln's staff may appear casual in defining exactly how they integrate community service learning into their daily routines, but their actions speak definitively: Just do it.

At the time this chapter was written, I was a reporter with the *Springfield Union News,* Springfield, Massachusetts.

Built in 1910, Lincoln School is in the North End section of Springfield, Massachusetts, a city of about 180,000 people. The school is a K–5 magnet school for computers and other technology. Until about five years ago, 98 percent of Lincoln's students were Hispanic. Through school choice and busing, the population is now about 48 percent Hispanic, 33 percent African American, 17 percent white, and 2 percent other (including Pakistani and Vietnamese).

Deliberately seeking "a sense of community" as part of a districtwide initiative, the Lincoln staff developed their community-service-learning program in 1987. Crime deeply permeated the school's inner-city neighborhood, an increasing number of students were being bused in—the number is currently at 55 percent—and there were the usual structural problems that come with an 84-year-old building constructed with no gym, cafeteria, or auditorium.

Good Citizenship

The school adopted "good citizenship" as their theme. While educating students about citizenship during language arts classes, teachers asked the students to nominate good citizens. Soon, a school "Wall of Fame" displayed dozens of written and drawn nominations of neighbors, staff, and other community members. Each class elected their good citizen from the nominations. These good citizens were then honored in a celebration called "Good Citizens on Parade." Everyone from the mayor and mounted police to the 4th grade band participated in the parade, which featured the "good citizens" the students had selected. Parents, grandparents, foster parents, camp counselors, and social workers marched along with children wearing Lincoln t-shirts and carrying banners and balloons.

Although this carefully crafted event occurred several years ago, in the spring of 1987, the school's culture of citizenship, caring, and service is still so pervasive that staff, students, parents and the neighbors expect it. In essence, the community-service-learning process made sense to the Lincoln School family because of their beliefs and teaching practices.

Daily Service Learning

"Service experiences don't always have to be some big production," said Mary Lou Pieczarka, a 5th grade teacher at the school since 1987, of bringing community service learning into the daily curriculum. "I think when you try and separate it and say, 'This is community service learning,' I'm not sure that children always have to be told that."

Pieczarka observed that reflection on the service experiences is an important part of the community-service-learning process. In a one-month period, for example, her students did a unit on homelessness and took a tour of the dietary wing of the nearby Baystate Medical Center before cooking meals for shelters; in math, boxes of macaroni and pounds of cheese became variables for equations; and in writing class, children wrote stories based on their interaction with people living on the street and with hospital professionals. "Using the thematic method, you don't have to say, 'I've got to do math, I've got to do English, now what am I going to do for community service learning?' It all fits together naturally," Pieczarka said.

Service learning at Lincoln continues on several levels. While a daily subject like chorus becomes a concert at the pediatric unit of the medical center, there is also service for the school community itself in which students strive to be "student of the week." Winners receive a certificate from the school store. An art class makes invitations for retired Lincoln School employees to return for a holiday party. A project with senior citizens from the neighborhood blends into geography as the students study the seniors' native countries.

A New Community Playground

Although Principal Figueredo was certainly proud to tick off an immediate list of the daily service projects going on at the time, one service project was clearly of major significance.

"You have to see the playground," he said, flashing photo after photo of the two-year, $30,000 project that involved neighborhood children of various ages, families, big and small businesses, a local television station, the police, and other municipal employees. "It's our pride and joy." Inspired by the goal of ownership, hundreds of people volunteered time, services, and funds to turn asphalt and dirt behind the school into the neighborhood's only playground. The project saved the city $9,000 and culminated on one rainy weekend when "people just kept working like nothing was coming out of the sky," Figueredo recalled, beaming.

The contributors included two of the area's largest businesses, Baystate Medical Center and Western Massachusetts Electric Co. (WMECO). The hospital's planning department designed the playground; and WMECO, who had offered to do the digging for the project, ultimately hired a professional excavator when their company's own equipment was unable to handle the hard dirt they encountered. A local television station donated film of the project for Lincoln's archives.

"I leave here at 5:30 or 6 o'clock at night—in the dark sometimes—and I look back and 15 or 16 kids are still on the playground," Figueredo said with a grin. Though the school could have acquired the funds through a budgetary appeal, "It was essential that it was a community project," he said. "As you know, it's been proven that if people build something in their neighborhood or backyard, it's going to be taken care of a little better than if someone was hired to do it."

Opening Doors

Educators at Lincoln have said that well-designed and-executed service-learning projects, with both service *and* reflection components, have opened doors for some students unable to excel in the traditional academic environment.

Figueredo loves to tell the story of one 4th grader—"not a stand-out in terms of academics"—who entered a citywide poster contest for Children's Safety Month. The winning poster would be displayed on a billboard on Interstate 91, the major highway running directly through the city. While waiting with the 38 other finalists to hear the contest results, the boy told Figueredo, "I'm not gonna win, Mr. Fig, I'm not gonna win."

And the principal said, "Don't worry about it, you're a winner already for coming up here." The student's poster, which warned children about drugs, was the winner. "He was so proud," Figueredo said.

First grade teacher Anita Palmeri, who has been at Lincoln since 1989, agreed that community service learning's value can reach far beyond the academics. "[The students] will see that community service can open doors for them, even if it's only to create a desire in their hearts and the knowledge that there are other things out there for them," she said, referring to the networking done in many service projects that can forge long-term relationships and lead to jobs later.

For school systems looking to mirror Lincoln's example, there is one challenge: The practice of weaving service projects into the daily life of the school is so second-nature that there is no formal policy or step-by-step training guide to go by (although the school system does have a K–8 community-service-learning curriculum that Pieczarka helped write). People at Lincoln have simply committed to making service part of the life of the school and integrating it into the educational process.

"We don't say everybody on the staff has to do a community-service-learning project. We encourage it, and say everybody should try to do something. They'll go to someone on the staff, to someone with the experience who will suggest ideas. And then they'll do it," said Figueredo of the informal way Lincoln's community-service-learning lifestyle is passed on to new teachers.

Pieczarka agreed that the school's culture of citizenship, caring, and community can only survive by its own hands. "I think it's important that we, as teachers, keep telling others who are doing it, 'You're helping other people, and kids are learning. That's the value.'"

6

Creating a School and Community Culture to Sustain Service Learning

Caroline Allam, Managing Director, KIDS Consortium,
Portland, Maine

You guys have always done this stuff for us. It's our town. We're the ones that are going to have to run the town after you old guys are gone. We ought to get a shot at making some decisions about the future (Lysen 1992, p. 8).

This strong sentiment came from a Bath Junior High School student who was working with peers, teachers, scientists, and other community members to conduct water quality tests on the Kennebec River in Maine. The statement reflects the desire and willingness of young people to work together, to assume responsibility and stewardship for their communities, and to acquire the knowledge and skills for informed decision making and citizenship. And it represents our collective hope for millions of other young adolescents.

According to the Carnegie Council on Adolescent Development (1989), the middle school years represent the last best chance for young people to choose a path toward productive and fulfilling lives. Those who make "fateful choices" may grow into adults "who are alienated from other people, who have low expectations for themselves, and for whom society has low expectations." Those who are "left behind" are likely to be the unhealthy, the addicted, the criminal, the violent, and the poor (Carnegie Council 1989).

What kind of school and community environment will help nurture the intellectual, social, and personal development of adolescents? How will we help young people become, as the Carnegie report suggests, intellectually reflective, productive, healthy, caring, and ethical citizens? The essence of an approach that responds to these demands must be a teaching and learning strategy that involves, engages, and empowers young people as workers, resources, and entrepreneurs in their schools and communities—and a school and community culture that values and sustains this approach.

Service Learning as Authentic Learning

Over the past four years, the KIDS (Kids Involved Doing Service) Consortium, a nonprofit organization in Portland, Maine, has helped schools and communities across New England design authentic educational strategies that involve students in tackling real-life problems as part of their English, science, social studies, and mathematics curriculum. Through a model called "KIDS as Planners," students not only learn subject matter in a meaningful and relevant context, but they also learn that they can make a difference as citizens and stewards of their schools and communities.

For example, middle school students have made important contributions to their towns by monitoring soil and water quality, documenting neighborhood and cultural history, conducting inventories of natural resources, developing and maintaining nature trails, designing playgrounds and green spaces, and mapping local wetlands. These projects provide a focus for integrating content and for helping students demonstrate the knowledge and skills outlined in Maine's Common Core of Learning, a bold vision of what all students should know and be able to do when they graduate from high school.

In addition, research has shown that opportunities for young people to participate in the life of their school and community help them develop problem-solving skills, social competence, autonomy, and a sense of purpose and future—attributes that enable them to bounce back from at-risk environments and lead healthy, productive lives. In other words, participation is prevention (Benard 1991).

The implementation of service learning, however, is often mired in concerns for logistics, such as training, supervision, transportation, and liability. The answers to these issues cannot be found in easy-to-read pamphlets. Most of the logistics are institutional barriers that will be addressed when a cultural shift occurs within schools and communities and service learning becomes the common modus operandi.

A City's Vision for Change

The city of Bath is a proud, old community on the coast of Maine, with a population of about 10,000. It is home to rich environmental treasures like the Kennebec River and the Merrymeeting Bay; a historic, revitalized, downtown shopping district; massive traffic problems on the Carlton Bridge; and an economy dependent on Bath Iron Works, the state's largest employer and the builder of the Aegis destroyer.

To encourage broad-based citizen participation in Bath's comprehensive planning process, the KIDS Consortium collaborated with City Planner Matthew Eddy to involve the community's most neglected resource—its youth. A plan is more than a piece of paper, according to Eddy; it is an expression of a city's vision of its future and its desired quality of life. This vision and the means to achieve it serve as a guide to influence all facets of community life and provide direction for future decision making.

The Bath Comprehensive Planning and Education Committee was created to coordinate efforts between planners and local educators. It included representatives from schools, Bath Iron Works, the Bath Historical Society, the Patten Free Library, the Maine Maritime Museum, the Chamber of Commerce, environmental groups, and city agencies. The committee's purpose was to establish a new rapport between those who were creating the guide to the city's future and those responsible for shaping the lives of the children who would lead it.

The committee created a new role and a new meaning for the word *community* in community service. Communities are not just places where kids serve, and service is not just a nice activity to keep kids busy. Representatives of public and private agencies, from the city electrician to the local historian, provide technical expertise to help students plan and carry out projects that have a long-term impact on the quality of life in the town. For example, one of the first projects in Bath teamed 7th graders with scientists at the Bigelow Laboratory, a privately owned marine research facility. Scientists taught students how to conduct water quality tests on the Kennebec River. Working in teams aboard a vessel furnished by Bath Iron Works, students determined water pollution levels in different sites of the city.

Based on their results, teams wrote recommendations to the city's Comprehensive Planning Committee regarding future land use—the lands the students will ultimately inherit. Students proposed rehabilitating a disused shipyard for recreational use, upgrading the town's Sewage Treatment Plant, and an immediate cleanup of polluted sites.

Based on a content analysis of letters to the committee, these students demonstrated an interest in community life (100 percent), a strong sense of responsibility to the community (86 percent), great enthusiasm for the learning process (73 percent), and a strong sense of efficacy (60 percent). Ultimately, the consensus that students were able to reach had a positive effect on members of the committee, who, up to that point, could reach no consensus (Kingsland 1993). All KIDS projects continue to be linked to the city's comprehensive plan.

The Comprehensive Planning and Education Committee, on the other hand, no longer exists, because it was successful in fulfilling its mission, to the point where educators were able to establish their own, independent working relationships with public and private officials to continue planning and carrying out community projects. The partnership ultimately led to a school board policy to endorse community-based learning for all K–12 students.

A School's Vision for Change

Service learning helps schools teach a core academic program for all students, the major tenet of all school restructuring initiatives. Indeed, a team of math, science, language arts, and social studies teachers at Bath Junior High School agreed that KIDS as Planners is completely compatible with their educational goals and objectives. To sustain and institutionalize this kind of teaching and learning, however, these teachers stressed the need for support from within the school. They would need time to plan, discuss, and integrate curriculum; longer and flexible blocks of instructional time; administrative leadership; involvement and support of parents; and assistance with logistical coordination of field visits (Kingsland 1993).

The institutionalization of service learning, from just a few teachers to a critical mass, from a special project to a sustainable teaching strategy, requires institutional change. Despite the fact that these highly motivated practitioners said that they would continue to implement the KIDS model and encourage their colleagues to become involved, sustaining and expanding faculty involvement would ultimately require a new vision of teaching and learning supported by changes in scheduling, organization, resources, assessment, and professional roles. Although service learning demands institutional changes and may even facilitate changes, it does not always guarantee them.

In the fall of 1994, Bath Junior High School formally became Bath Middle School. Over the past two years, a middle school committee composed of parents, teachers, and administrators defined the guiding principles that would transform the school into "a place where people want to be." The principles include a core curriculum of reading, writing, mathematics, science, and social studies for all students; instructional grouping that reflects validated research; interdisciplinary teaching; flexible blocks of instructional time; small communities of learning guided by caring adults who know each child well; parent involvement; and common planning time for teaching teams. In addition, the committee recommended that "citizenship and community service be emphasized as part of the educational process."

To facilitate these changes, the school district and the middle school agreed to participate in KIDSNET (Kids Involved Doing Service in New England Towns), a three-year national demonstration project funded by the Corporation for National Service. Sponsored by the KIDS Consortium, KIDSNET will build the capacity of five school districts in Maine, Vermont, and Connecticut to use KIDS as Planners as a vehicle for helping students meet high academic standards based on each state's Common Core of Learning. The leadership team for the project—a team of four teachers at Bath Middle School, plus the district's substance abuse counselor—recruited 14 colleagues into the KIDS process, representing about one-third of the faculty and 385 students. Each team researched and identified an interdisciplinary project that could be carried out across teams or with the local elementary school and high school. Examples include composting lunchroom waste, designing a school courtyard for outdoor activities, developing a management plan for 135 acres of pristine public land known as Butler Cove, and renovating the McMann Field Complex for athletic and recreational use. People representing such interests as the Bath Department of Parks and Cemeteries and the school hot lunch program will serve as critical resources to help students research, design, and carry out solutions to significant problems in their school and community environments.

Ultimately, KIDS will be sustained not only by institutional changes at the middle school but by the ownership of teachers as frontline advocates and leaders for change. KIDSNET is neither a collection of isolated KIDS projects nor a program run in the school by an outside agency. Instead, it demonstrates the value of capacity building, creating new roles and responsibilities for teachers. For example, Paula Evans is a veteran 7th grade teacher who has become a liaison and facilitator for KIDS as Planners projects. As a leader of a teaching team, she has recruited her own team into the process, consulted with other teams to develop projects, coordinated projects across schools, trained teachers from other school systems, and participated in professional workshops and conferences to facilitate staff development activities at the school. Over the next three years, KIDSNET will create a cadre of local advocates, like Paula, including teachers, administrators, students, and community members, who facilitate the institutionalization of the KIDS model in many ways:

• as a participant in a school or community-based network that provides a forum for sharing and support

• as an on-site facilitator who coaches the involvement of teachers new to the KIDS process

• as a trainer, facilitator, or presenter at a KIDS workshop or local faculty meeting

• as a mentor to a student-teacher

• as a consultant who communicates with interested audiences beyond their own school systems

• as a presenter of the KIDS model at a state, regional, or national conference

• as an author of an article on the KIDS model for local or professional audiences

• as an organizer or planner of any of these activities

Service learning not only demands changes within schools and communities; but, by changing roles and relationships among students, teachers, administrators, parents, and community members, service learning also helps to facilitate cultural shifts and foster collegiality, enthusiasm, recognition, high expectations, responsibility, and an ethic of caring. These cultural shifts within our communities and institutions will ultimately help us achieve the most important transition of all—to the creation of a culture that encourages and values youth at the turning point of their lives.

References

Benard, B. (1991). *Fostering Resiliency in Kids: Protective Factors in the Family, School, and Community.* Portland, Ore.: Western Regional Center for Drug-Free Schools and Communities.

Carnegie Council on Adolescent Development. Task Force on the Education of Young Adolescents. (1989). *Turning Points: Preparing American Youth for the 21st Century.* Washington, D.C.: Carnegie Council on Adolescent Development.

Kingsland, S.F. (1993). *KIDS as Planners Evaluation 1991–1993.* Report submitted to Maine Office of Substance Abuse in accordance with requirements for the Community Youth Activity Program Block Grants. Portland, Me.: KIDS Consortium, Inc.

Lysen, J. (March 1992). "Kids as Planners." *Maine Progressive*, p. 8.

7

How Do We Make a Difference in Our Community?

Len Solo, Principal, Graham & Parks Alternative Public School, Cambridge, Massachusetts

We are witnessing a profound loss of community in the United States. People have turned away from caring about others to caring about themselves. Evidence of this loss, accelerated from a trend in the early 1960s, has become a major feature of life in the latter part of the 20th century. Loss of community is seen everywhere: the number of homeless people on the streets; the number of children living in poverty; the physical and verbal violence everywhere; the rise in intolerance of groups toward each other; the increase in racial incidents; townspeople, even neighbors, not caring for or even knowing each other; the litter on the roads and in the streets; the decline of services available to the poor; and the sense of loneliness and isolation felt by many. At Graham & Parks Alternative Public School, we believe that we *can* and *must* teach students how to develop community, to be a part of a community, and to live in communities.

Graham & Parks Alternative Public School is a K–8 school in Cambridge, Massachusetts. Three hundred and seventy students participate in the school program, which is guided by an open education philosophy. Len Solo has been the principal since 1974.

Creating Empowered Communities Through Apprenticeships

One of the goals at our school is to develop a community within our middle school program. One aspect of creating community is to *empower* people: All people in the community need to know that they not only can but must be involved in developing the place in which they work or live. Staff, working as a team, develop projects, schedules, curriculum, or activities that they think will improve the program. Students have a voice in developing the program through the School Council and a biweekly Community Meeting, and parents provide input through monthly meetings. Graham & Parks uses many other community-building strategies: getting everyone to work hard at developing attitudes of caring and respect; focusing on making a safe place, with positive strategies for dealing with conflict; and designing activities that require people to work cooperatively. Activities include adventure-type programs away from the school, going to movies, mountain climbing, and visiting museums.

Middle school students are developmentally ready to move out into their communities, to go beyond home and school, and to grow up and out into the larger world. Consequently, at Graham & Parks, we believe that we need to teach students how to live effectively in a community. This belief led us, in the mid-1970s, to develop an apprenticeship program. Students were placed in as many as 60 different sites in the Cambridge area, including hospitals, auto repair shops, animal hospitals, day care centers, restaurants, banks, law offices, architectural firms, police stations, public works agencies, and other sites. In this program, through the late 1980s, apprenticeships were available only to 8th grade students.

Planning the Community Service Project

In 1991, we changed the nature and scope of this program into a Community Service Project involving all 7th and 8th graders, including our Haitian bilingual students. Students serve an agency, learn about the work conducted in the agency, and investigate an important person in the agency and how this person contributes to the life of the agency. We made this significant change for important reasons: The apprenticeship program was loosely connected to the in-school curriculum, and we wanted to have all activities in our total program integrated with several basic ideas and themes we were developing.

The planning process for the Community Service Project involved staff, students, and parents. The staff meets three times a week; in these meetings, the staff initiated a new direction for the entire middle school program. Their vision was to redesign the program around themes, which included figuring out how to integrate curriculum, structuring longer class periods and a more flexible schedule, thinking of how to have much more student involvement in learning through project-oriented interactive curriculums, and having exhibitions of students' work.

To achieve this vision, staff and students discussed ideas during the biweekly Community Meeting. Here, students became involved in helping to plan the new program. Staff discussed with students what they were thinking, and the students decided to explore this new direction with the staff. Simultaneously, we held several evening discussions with parents about the idea. Although they expressed concerns about the 7th grade students' involvement, the parents agreed that the change would be a positive thing for the school and the students. Thus, the school community developed consensus to initiate the pilot project. We then approached many community agencies about our idea, and almost all agreed to participate. Each site agreed to provide our students with *meaningful* work and to assign an employee—a mentor—to work closely with our students and staff.

Our Community Service Project is currently under the direction of a coordinator—one of our part-time instructional aides whose hours were increased to do this job from a grant. The coordinator has multi-layered responsibilities that include selecting appropriate community work/service sites; training site coordinators; getting information about these sites to staff, students, and parents; and helping students choose a site, arranging transportation (if needed), supervising students at the sites, passing on information to teachers so it can be incorporated into the in-school curriculum, and solving the hundreds of little problems that occur in this type of project.

During the past year, the coordinator did extensive training of the site mentors: meeting with them individually and helping them understand how they need to teach and work with students. We also had an evening meeting with all mentors, relying on the experienced mentors to help us answer questions and give advice to the new mentors. Finally, the coordinator developed a handbook of information for the mentors. This training proved to be effective and helped us see that this is an essential ingredient for students to have a successful community service experience.

Each teacher in the program and the assistant principal work with the project. They help design it, meet with students, help students choose sites, visit students at the sites several times a week, develop the curriculum-integration activities, help develop the exhibit, and assess the various pieces of the project.

Community Service Learning in the Humanities

As a result of the planning and teamwork, Graham & Parks now has a humanities curriculum with double-blocked classes that integrate language arts and social studies. Because we have multigraded classes of 7th and 8th graders, we need to have two humanities curriculums. During the first year (1991–92), our Community Service Project focused on the theme, "How Do People Make a Difference in Their Community?"—part of a unit in our year-long 7th and 8th grade curriculum, "Facing History and Ourselves/Civil Rights Movements." This curriculum deals with issues like the power of the individual and governments, involved and noninvolved citizens, how individuals become leaders, and how people can organize and work together for change, as well as issues connected with the Holocaust and with the civil rights movements in the United States.

In the second year (1992–93), we focused on the essential question, "What Makes America America?"—a study of American history from the 1830s to the present, using imigration as a lens, and focusing on the history of Cambridge. First, students studied themselves and their family backgrounds; then, they studied various waves of immigration to this country, with an emphasis on the Cambridge area. Students studied how the city has changed over time due to immigration and industrialization; how it went from a small, almost rural community to a city; how industries grew and changed; and where people live, the buildings, the types of work done, and other characteristics.

In 1991–92, all 7th and 8th graders were involved in community service work that extended over a period of 10 weeks and was broken into 2 weeks of preparation activities, 6 weeks of actual work (for half a day per week) in a community agency or business; and 2 weeks of follow-up activities.

In 1992–93, we changed this format so that students worked for five hours a day for five consecutive days, going out to their jobs after spending about 15 minutes in school preparing for the day and reviewing the previous day's work. We found that this new time structure allowed us to sharpen and focus the program. Over the years, it is our intent to experiment with time formats to see the strengths and weaknesses of each before we settle on a final format.

Authentic Learning in the Community

Students do a series of short-term and long-term investigative projects that result in various kinds of exhibitions of their learning. Exhibitions include research articles, plays, puppet shows, models, original poems, a cartoon-type book, and other creative venues—from dramatizations of *Animal Farm*, to civil rights activities, to studying one's own family.

The projects begin with students' brainstorming areas of concern in the community in preparation for their community service activities. In 1992, these concerns included health care, legal services, homelessness, elderly people, consumer protection, hunger, community education, and the environment. All students (usually in pairs) are placed at a job site falling within one of these areas, and curriculum is developed to support the learning at the work sites, as well as to enhance students' research, analytical, and mathematical skills. One of our concerns is helping students understand how a community works: how the separate jobs, businesses, agencies, organizations, and educational institutions connect.

Placement sites include day care centers, the police department, homeless shelters, the public library, the rent control office, the Consumer Affairs Office, the Council on Aging, the Multi-Cultural Arts Center, the Public Works Department, and other city agencies. For the second year's curriculum, we also used many business sites such as small stores. Examples include a plumbing/heating contractor, local newspapers, architects, and pet stores. Usually, we have 40–60 sites available for our students.

Over the years, it is also our intent to experiment with sites: from placing one or two students at a wide variety of sites, to focusing the students and the curriculum on a few select sites, to focusing on one site or one type of site. In our first year, there were three parts to the project: three hours a week of work in a community service organization, curriculum work in school exploring issues in the community, and a community service project done by each student.

In their community service agency, the students explore the world of work. For many students, it is the first time they have had such an opportunity. The students also explore their agency: who works there, what they do, how they do it, whom they serve, how effective they are, and other questions about careers. This work experience also includes opportunities for students to develop interaction skills, such as introducing one's self, asking questions, clarifying instructions, and starting conversations—all challenging issues for early adolescents.

The staff developed an integrated, interdisciplinary curriculum that uses the Community Service Project as an experiential way to learn content skills. The initial set of activities involve social skills development; these occur before the students go out to do community work. The staff developed mini-lessons, using discussions and role-plays, to practice the necessary social skills for the students' work sites. The following activities are also included:

• Each student is required to explore a community issue through a major research paper. Sources include both primary and secondary information, such as literature from the job site, interviews, newspaper articles, and library research. The teachers, job site supervisors, and the librarian help the students find these sources of information. Students regularly meet across homeroom groupings, with their focus group, to share and discuss their research and experiences.

• Each student must read a biography of a person who made a difference in his or her community. Students then write a short summary, responding to how that person made a difference and why the person made particular choices. Every student develops a book cover for this report. A designer from a major publisher comes in to classes to share her techniques with the students.

• Students make floor plans to scale of their work sites. This activity fits into the unit on ratio and proportion in math and is done during class in the computer lab.

• Throughout their volunteer experiences in the community, students keep a daily log reflecting on many levels, both affective and cognitive. Each daily log entry is structured by a key question from the teachers; yet students are encouraged to write any additional comments about their work.

• After the first few days of work, students are asked to write a "five-senses" poem that should convey a real "sense" of their workplaces. Here is one such poem:

klackety-klack echoing
empty clean hallways
slightly audible

superficial
voices muttering
meaningless

old
near-expired dinosaur
screeching paper out
in the corner

hastily oversalty
light lunch of lost folders

rough worn edges
bent
torn
overstuffed
filled with their lives
images inner ailments

cold
perfect
unbreakable glass
shock-lining

peephole in a heavy tent-flap
revealing a metal monster
looking into the mind
patient
oh so patient

place of the mind
hold things eyes can't see
lock away images so important
called up when needed
locked up for thirteen years
until Tommy trips again

• During the period of time when students are out at their work/service site, they are to design a poster that shows where the materials at the job site come from and where they end up. This aspect of the curriculum is monitored by the science and resource room teachers and is part of a unit on recycling and ecology.

• At the end of this unit, students are asked to develop an exhibit about their work experience that demonstrates what they did and what they learned. Using large display boards or table-top displays, students develop an exhibition to show what they learned at their work sites. These involve pictures, videos, drawings, floor plans, excerpts from their logs and research papers, the poster or poem, and models. On a given day and evening, all the students' exhibits are displayed in classrooms and the school's halls for the work site supervisors, community leaders, teachers, parents, and fellow students to view. Each class in the school visits the exhibit. The 7th and 8th graders explain to the visitors their various projects and the impact of the Community Service Project on their thinking. This is a wonderful community celebration that allows students to show off their learning and to grow in the process.

• Finally, students are asked to organize and implement a community action activity. Each student or groups of students develop projects that give something back to the community. These community action projects are done after all other activities and usually take over a month to complete. The following are some activities developed for the pilot year of our project:

Clothing, food, and toy drive for shelters and hospitals
Book and magazine drive for a homeless shelter
Big books and games given to day care centers
Educational display made of the city's agencies
A recycling program at a nearby school
Money collection for UNICEF
Educational environmental displays created
Lessons on the city hospital and fire department for 1st and 2nd
    graders

A similar set of activities was developed for the second year's curriculum, "What Makes America America?" These included daily focus questions for students, a summary essay, an essay on how the work site helps make the city work, a model or symbol of the work site that is placed on a room-sized floor map of the city, and written interviews with their mentor.

Evaluation of Community Service Projects

Evaluation is an ongoing aspect of the project. First, staff members visit work sites and observe students in their work. Staff solicite verbal feedback from the site supervisor at each visit. At the end of the work experience, a written, final evaluation, developed by the school staff, is completed by the site supervisor and is mailed to the school. As noted previously, the students keep a daily log of their activities, and these are read by the coordinator and the students' homeroom teachers. All students' productions—research papers, poems, floor plans, and other work—are assessed by the teachers. At the end of the project, the coordinator meets with the students and gives them feedback and "debriefs" them about the total experience. Because all staff are involved in the project, evaluation is the subject of one of the three weekly team meetings during the length of the project. Problems, course corrections, individual students or sites, and other issues are the subjects of this discussion and shared decision making.

For example, the structure of the program changed in 1992–93 because of what we learned from the initial experience. Students told us that some of the work was not meaningful and that they did not feel themselves making a difference. Therefore, we changed the time to one full week of work at a site. This change compelled the site mentors to plan more carefully for our students and to really get involved in their work.

Students' daily logs, essays, and summaries are valuable tools in the evaluation of our program. For example, here is how one bilingual student viewed her work at the Margaret Fuller House, a neighborhood center that includes a day care center and a tutoring center among its activities:

> When I got to school, my teacher said, "Everybody is going to their work sites today. Some of you will be driven by parents."

> When I got there, I introduced myself to a woman named Sherlie. Sherlie told me that my supervisor was not there, so she asked me to answer the phone and take messages. She explained how to do it. I answered the phone a lot of times.

> The second Wednesday that I went to the Margaret Fuller House, nobody was there, but then I saw a lady getting out of her car, and she opened the door. I asked her, "Are you Iona?" She said, "Yes," and we went inside.

> I started telling her about the job site and she said, "Oh, yeah! You're from the Graham & Parks School, right?"

> "That's right," I answered. Then Sherlie walked in. I asked her, "May I interview you?" She said, "Yes."

> We went upstairs, and she showed me her office and a lot of stuff. I started to ask her some questions, and she said, "Before you begin to ask me questions, let me tell you some things about the Margaret Fuller House." In about two seconds she showed me a schedule.

> Margaret Fuller House is open on Mondays through Fridays, 10 a.m. to 10 p.m. She said, "We have an after-school [program] for children ages 5 to 12 years old. And then we have the Parents' Aide Program where individuals from the community work with other parents from the community who are experiencing stress. This is to help them deal with their stress so they don't abuse or neglect their children."

> So I got all the answers to my questions from her telling me about the place. Then Iona walked in. She said, "Sherlie, did you show her all the things in the Margaret Fuller House?"

"No," she said. Then Iona showed me all of the things in the place. After, she said, "One more thing I forgot to show you is in the basement."

"What is it?" I asked her.

She said, "It's a Day Care. If you want to work in it, you can." I thought about that being my work site. It would be great because I love working with kids. So, I told her that I would love to work at their Day Care Center.

It's located in a large room like a house filled with kids. There is a big couch, a big table, a lot of chairs, games, toys, and books like the *Cat in the Hat* and *Green Eggs and Ham*.

I taught the kids the alphabet, colors, and read aloud to them. When we went outside, I helped them get on the slide. The kids liked when I was around because I put on their coats for them when they were all going outside.

I learned there that you have to think ahead about how to organize activities or you have to run after the kids all the time. For example, if you tell them to come to snack, you have to ring a bell and say, "Snack time!" and they will be at the table, because if you don't, they all will be hiding.

I'd like to be a day care teacher because it is fun working with kids and you can also learn a lot from them. For example, if you have a little brother, from those kids you can learn a lot about what kids are like.

Day care centers make a difference by helping kids to be smart for kindergarten. It is also a good place for kids to go while parents have to be at work, and it is also a safe place for your child to be.

* * *

Is our project working? Are our students really becoming active, involved citizens? It is far too early for us to answer these questions because we won't have solid information until the students become adults. It is our sense, though, that our community service project is having a significant effect on our students and that we are indeed teaching them about their responsibilities as citizens. Certainly, the program has affected how we provide educational experiences for our students.

8

High School: Service Learning and a Caring School Community

Janice M. Reeder, Principal, Gig Harbor High School,
Gig Harbor, Washington

We become just by doing just acts, temperate by doing temperate acts, brave by doing brave acts. By extension we become compassionate by doing compassionate acts, caring by doing caring acts and good citizens by acting as good citizens (Conrad 1988).

Service is an integral part of the curricular, athletic, and leadership program at Gig Harbor High School:

• The Spanish classes wrote and translated children's stories into Spanish, and the drawing class illustrated them. These books were donated to the Martin Luther King Shelter for homeless families to encourage Hispanic parents to read to their children.

• Gig Harbor students recently received a national award for their work with homeless children.

• The biology and ecology classes run a science lab at the neighboring elementary school five days a week.

• Members of the football team watch Monday night football with senior citizens at convalescent centers.

• Leadership students are mentors for at-risk elementary school children.

• Business education students serve as bookkeepers for FISH, the local food bank.

Gig Harbor High School is a four-year, suburban high school of 1,300 students from predominantly white middle-class families in Gig Harbor, Washington State.

- Drama students presented a production dealing with the homeless as a fund raiser, donated the ticket money to a homeless shelter, and invited people from the shelter to attend the play.

As teachers and students connect classroom learning to community concerns, they do it purposefully, knowing that they are making a difference. In our school and community, we no longer wait for someone else to do things. We step forward. In the halls, in the classrooms, and in the community, students now offer to help whenever someone needs assistance.

Service Learning Benefits the Entire Learning Community.

Service learning is helping us do the right thing, not only for the Gig Harbor community and for students, but for staff. Service learning is bringing what teachers believe and value into our work, thereby making it more meaningful. To plan and implement the process, teachers have restructured the school day. Teachers now feel empowered to do things because they have a structure to support them. Because they and their students are involved with activities that are valued by the community, they receive recognition for their work through positive newspaper articles. Teachers now feel increased pride as they reach beyond themselves to help others.

Service learning is helping us do the right thing for the school. Students are now willing to step forward and do whatever it takes to make the school work. They are co-partners with the teachers in helping to build an effective school community, whether that means putting up signs in the community or helping to solve problems that arise around the school.

Service learning is helping us do the right thing for the community. The community now comes to the school when it needs help.

Restructuring a high school does not happen overnight. Our service learning started with a few teachers' implementing a variety of projects; over time, it has grown to become one of the main components of our school reform process. We have developed a strategy of teaching that has made service a part of the culture of the school itself—not a class, not a project, but a part of the everyday way of doing business in the school.

Service learning is applicable to most aspects of school reform and is, therefore, a powerful vehicle for restructuring schools. When schools implement service-learning programs and are able to graduate students prepared to contribute to their community, with skills for employment, these schools will have developed the hearts as well as the minds of their graduates.

Service Learning Is a Powerful Tool for School Reform.

Our school reform plan required that we create a vision. Although many people view the creation of a vision as an essential starting place for restructuring a school, it's difficult to align a comprehensive vision and a strategy powerful enough to achieve that vision. As parents, community, teachers, and students developed a vision for their school and its graduates, they realized that they wanted their school to be a caring community and their graduates to be caring, responsible citizens. They agreed that service learning is a powerful strategy to help us work toward our vision.

Our students regularly extend themselves to help others by working at the local food bank, mentoring in elementary classrooms, or producing newsletters for nonprofit and community agencies. After participating in service projects, students talk of an increased sense of social responsibility; they feel appreciated by the community and, as a result, more positive about themselves.

Because the real indicators of our success as a high school are the actions of young people after they graduate, we're delighted to see that many graduates continue their commitment to making the community a better place. One of our graduates, for example, has established a volunteer center at her college and has designed a cross-aged mentoring program that currently involves more than 150 students.

The reform movement calls for teachers to make learning meaningful and relevant for students. And to this end, as the school staff worked to define the primary skills and desired competencies, they realized that some important outcomes are difficult to realize in a traditional classroom. Service learning is a proven teaching strategy to achieve performance-based outcomes.

As they perform a service activity that applies curriculum concepts, students can see how learning applies to their real lives. For example, accounting students, working with the local food bank, apply classroom accounting principles while doing real work for this community agency. Biology students monitoring a stream for the Environmental Protection Agency are doing real work to improve the environment as they learn ecology concepts. The payoff in such projects is that students feel good about contributing to their community, and this feeling will likely carry over into their adult lives, ensuring ongoing contributions to their local communities. In addition, the agencies have the opportunity to gain a positive impression of today's youth.

Service Learning Is a Valuable Tool for Youth Development.

Students must learn to process information as they prepare for a future in which information itself changes at an alarming pace. Teaching students problem-solving and thinking skills is critical to their ability to function effectively in this future. Service-learning activities allow students to learn and develop problem-solving and decision-making skills.

The business community cites the inability to function as a member of a team as a major skill deficiency of students entering the work force. Many of our service projects teach students teamwork. Science students, for example, worked together to design and teach science lessons to elementary students. In addition to enhancing their own understanding of science concepts, the students worked collaboratively to develop a creative way to "turn younger students on" to science.

High school art students worked with a neighboring elementary classroom to develop a clay mural for the elementary school. The older students learned how to be hosts for the younger students and, by explaining techniques to their elementary partners, solidified their own understanding of the skills.

The public's demand for schools' accountability is leading to new and alternate forms of assessment of skills, another issue of reform. School goals have changed so radically that standardized testing is no longer an effective assessment method. Schools are examining portfolio assessments, in which students collect examples from their service work to demonstrate competence and application of course content skills. Written reflection following participation in community service, for example, is a clear demonstration of writing and thinking skills; it reveals the capacity to apply course content and the degree to which students have gained a sense of social responsibility and self-esteem. As the public increases its pressure on schools for accountability, schools need to be more organized about identifying and assessing student performances.

Service Learning Is Useful—But How Do We Find Time to Do It?

The inability to break away from the traditional schedule of six or seven periods each day has restricted reform efforts in many secondary schools. Rushing through six subjects in a row each day has never made much sense, but most teachers have strongly resisted changing the schedule.

Recent analysis of successful change efforts has shown that people change when they see a need for change and when they know how to change. The need to change the high school schedule is not clearly felt by most teachers. However, school reform efforts are not only calling for them to change the school schedule but, more significantly, to change their teaching and the curriculum. Service learning became the incentive for teachers at Gig Harbor to embrace a restructuring of the school day. As teachers came to believe in service learning and increased their service activities, they saw the need for longer instructional blocks of time. Service learning caused teachers to support change in the schedule.

As more and more teachers at Gig Harbor High School became involved in service learning, they found that 50–60-minute periods were restricting students' ability to be involved in significant projects. Teachers demanded and got 100-minute instructional blocks, and they learned how to use the longer blocks to teach more effectively. Teachers expanded their service activities to implement the types of projects described earlier. Advisory blocks and team-planning time were also scheduled into the new day. To encourage students to get involved in significant issues, the school established an advisory period that is held twice a week to give service clubs and leadership groups time to effectively implement their programs. In addition, a Leadership for Service class was created that organized service activities for students, with a student assisting a teacher in making all the community arrangements.

Service Learning Works.

Service transforms everyday acts. Many schools have long supported food and clothing drives, but students rarely experienced them as service. By deliberately using the term "service" when we speak of helping each other in even the simplest kindness, we begin to change our school community. A commitment to service also helped us develop a pervasive culture of caring within the school.

Effecting change in the culture of a school community is no small task. It takes a serious commitment at all levels. We have found that service learning is a process that grows rapidly and continuously as people begin to use it and realize its tremendous potential for youth. We must continue the growth process as we train, support, and celebrate the successes of our youth through community service learning.

Reference

Conrad, D. (1988). *All the Difference: Youth Service in Minnesota*. St. Paul: University of Minnesota.

9

Service Learning Honors Cultural Diversity

Wokie Roberts-Weah, Director of National Programs,
National Youth Leadership Council, St. Paul, Minnesota

Serving one another has historically been a core value of many cultures around the world. In recent years, a growing number of U.S. classrooms and schools have recognized service as a powerful way to connect youth to their communities and cultural identities, to help preserve service as a value, and to enhance learning opportunities. Learning principles of service, cultural relevance, and responsibility through service-oriented curriculums helps students understand, appreciate, and value the rich histories in our diverse populations.

Currently, many U.S. schools and districts are developing curriculum models incorporating service learning and multicultural concepts. These programs result in positive learner outcomes, ranging from enhanced cultural empowerment, to a better-developed sense of community pride, to knowledge of how to implement social action. Like other service-learning initiatives in the United States, schools in New Mexico, Pennsylvania, and Minnesota have attained such outcomes for their students through cultural empowerment, cultural mobilization, cultural exploration, and social action.

Cultural Empowerment

The cultural-empowerment model uses service learning as the foundation for exploring the cultural roots of service. In Acoma, New Mexico, for example, Sky City Community School developed *A amuu htsii* ("For the Love of Mother Earth," in the Keres language), a multiyear curriculum project relating academic disciplines to the concept of preserving the community. Its goals are to deepen students' understanding of Acoma's history and to help them learn environmental concepts that will likely affect Pueblo life in the future. The curriculum provides opportunities for elementary school students to study soil formation through the science curriculum, conduct community nature walks as part of a social studies class, and maintain a journal of their findings for language arts. Community service is integrated into the curriculum through the annual refurbishing of Saint Estevan's Church for Feast Day. Students remove litter from the school grounds, and they construct tribal calendars that are shared with younger children. Learning objectives for the *A amuu htsii* curriculum are intricately linked to traditional Native American values, such as nourishing the earth, serving the community, and maintaining balance and harmony as part of daily life.

Cultural Mobilization

The cultural-mobilization model engages students from diverse cultural backgrounds in meaningful community service projects to heighten multicultural understanding and encourage cooperative action Northeast Middle School—Minneapolis' largest and most culturally diverse middle school—used this approach when they transformed an unused portion of the schoolyard into a functional community Gathering Place. The area is complete with performance stage, amphitheater, rock garden, and information kiosk. The Gathering Place Project, which had multidisciplinary applications, used art as a creative field for exploring diversity issues, math to teach basic measuring skills, industrial arts to construct picnic benches, and science to teach students how to build an environmentally sensitive sculpture garden. Today, the Gathering Place hosts community education classes, neighborhood meetings, and music performances. Student artwork on the walls of the information kiosk and concrete floor of the amphitheater documents the importance and range of different cultural groups represented in the school.

Discussions about one's family, socioeconomic status, and cultural identity are natural outgrowths of the preparation, action, and reflection phases of the cultural mobilization model These activities can be the start of a lifelong journey toward multicultural understanding and self-discovery.

Cultural Exploration

The cultural-exploration model combines concepts of diversity and service learning to increase students' understanding of the history and culture of their community. In Phoenixville, Pennsylvania, 4th graders from Schuylkill Elementary became part of a real intergenerational learning experience by working collaboratively with the Kiwanis Club to produce *A Phoenixville Journey, Past, and Future*. The publication, which was subsequently shared with school districts throughout the state, brings to life the history, sites, and legacy of a small rural community in Pennsylvania. Production of the book, which involved exploration of 15 student-selected historical landmarks, gave Schuylkill elementary students and the community at large a chance to learn about and be proud of their community.

Social Action and Change

In Minneapolis, Minnesota, the Forum Project of Webster Open School combined media technology, the performing arts, and service learning. This project positively demonstrates how service learning can be used to change students' attitudes about diversity. After participating in intensive awareness and prejudice-reduction training, 80 middle school students experienced a significant gain in multicultural understanding and awareness. Newly acquired skills and knowledge were put to good use when the Forum students produced an interactive video series on prejudice reduction. Today that series is a permanent part of the Webster Open School video library and is used to educate younger students, particularly those in suburban communities, on positive ways to directly address racism and sexism.

* * *

Despite differences in approaches and intended outcomes of these curricular models, all were developed by the schools, working in collaboration with their communities. The models include activities valued by young people, and the programs involve active and inquiry-based learning.

When we honor ties that bind people to the history of their ancestors in projects like *A amuu htsii*, we move one step closer to teaching students about the process of values formation in different cultures. Cultural-mobilization models, like the Gathering Place of Northeast Middle School, can help students develop respect for the culture of all learners by working together on issues of common interest. As the Phoenixville example illustrates, in-depth research studies of community development can highlight the contributions of many different ethnic groups and increase understanding of complex community issues. Social-action projects, such as the one in Minneapolis that focuses on racism, provide opportunities for students to examine their beliefs, in comparison to those of other cultural, socioeconomic, and religious groups.

In these times of dramatic shifts in national school demographic patterns, we must respond to the challenge of making stronger connections to the cultural roots of all students. According to James Banks (1994) in *Multiethnic Education*, demographers now project that nearly half of U.S. school-aged youth will be students of color by 2020. It will become critically important for schools to employ a teaching staff that works effectively with a complex mix of races, cultures, and languages. Understanding and help from the community will be essential to bridge this gap.

As we seek new approaches to make learning more relevant and accessible to students who learn in a variety of ways, service learning is an important instructional methodology that allows us to maintain academic standards, involve students from all cultural backgrounds, and bring greater understanding and meaning of the attributes of various cultures.

References

Baldwin, A. (April 1977). "Tests Can Under-Predict: A Case Study." *Phi Delta Kappan* 58, 8: 620–621.

Banks, J. (1994). *Multiethnic Education: Theory and Practice.* 3rd ed. Boston: Allyn and Bacon.

Bennett, C. (1990). *Comprehensive Multicultural Education: Theory and Practice.* 2nd ed. Boston: Allyn and Bacon.

Cairn, R., and W. Roberts. (Spring 1993). "Addressing Issues of Race and Culture Through Service-Learning." *The Generator* 13, 1: 14–17..

Hall, M. (Fall 1993). "Service Learning in Native Communities: The Generator School Project." *Journal of Navajo Education* 11, 1: 3–6.

Part III

Service Experiences Encourage Teachers to Facilitate Learning

10

Middle School: Intergenerational Experiences Support Teaching and Learning

Lisa Laplante, Project Manager,
Community Service Learning Center, Springfield, Massachusetts

Community service learning closes the gap between youth and the elderly. Through community service learning, students not only study subjects like English, history, and science, but also gain perspective about the lives of our senior population. This arrangement allows students to dispel false assumptions as they learn about the lives of seniors, and, in the process, develop empathy. Using an intergenerational theme, teachers satisfy several educational objectives by offering activities that facilitate both cognitive and affective learning.

Veteran teachers involved in this type of project constantly emphasize the power of bringing seniors together with youth. For many teachers, the relationship formed with the senior partners becomes a powerful vehicle for conveying preestablished curriculum. The testimony that follows demonstrates how community service learning affects both learner outcomes and instructional strategy.

The two schools discussed in this chapter are middle-level schools serving small urban communities, with a small proportion of rural students. Students in both schools represent varied ethnic and socioeconomic groups. Agawam Middle School, in Agawam, Massachusetts, has an enrollment of about 590 students; West Springfield Junior High School, in West Springfield, Massachusetts, serves about 700 students.

Living History

Jeanne Forgette and Louis Spiro, teachers at Agawam Middle School in Agawam, Massachusetts, used community service learning to teach history. In this project, students visited a senior center, where they conducted interviews that they eventually compiled into a class book entitled *Living History*. The students then gave the book as a gift to the people at the senior center. In addition, students performed a radio show for their older friends, featuring songs and commercials from eras through which their audience had lived. Both Forgette and Spiro were enthusiastic about the "fantastic" outcomes of the project. Forgette notes that students became more aware of elderly people. Because many of her students had limited contact with senior citizens, this opportunity allowed the children to be exposed to many different lifestyles of senior citizens. According to Forgette, the best part of the project was students' increased level of comfort and caring toward the elderly.

Spiro echoes Forgette's sentiments by noting both the academic and emotional outcomes of their project. He states:

> The aim was to have the students write a book. So they learned to write. The hidden curriculum had to do with learning about the elderly. Most of the students (50–80 percent) never dealt with elderly [people]. Some didn't have grandparents alive or nearby. Even if they had grandparents, the students gained a greater appreciation for the problems of the elderly.

The instruction used by Forgette and Spiro honored teamwork at all levels. The two teachers worked closely, both contributing equally; it was a "true partnership" that continues today. The teachers also involved students in planning, an approach that required the teachers to stay flexible so as to meet diverse student needs. Forgette and Spiro observe:

> You can teach the same thing day to day, but when you do projects like this, it motivates you, it invigorates you and keeps you young. It involves experimenting and letting kids go to see what they can do.

The teachers guided the process by first working with students to set up questions that would lead to specific learning outcomes and then by helping the class compose essays based on the student findings. In addition, the teachers spent time preparing the students for what they could expect from the elders in terms of energy level, speaking, and behaviors. The community-service-learning project required that the teachers change certain aspects of the curriculum to accommodate the service activities. Interview skills, general behaviors toward elders, and compiling books are specific areas included to enable students to perform the service activity.

Forgette stresses that this project made learning more relevant. She says she felt challenged to "do the real thing, to get out there!" She adds, "Anytime you can go out of the school there is a lot of learning involved." Community service learning made her "more aware of the contribution children can make to a community. . . . Although ten years old, they can still accomplish some very wonderful things."

Project BRIDGES

Maureen Perkins, Gala-Ann McInerny, and Ann Bongiorni, teachers at West Springfield Junior High School in West Springfield, Massachusetts, led their students through an intergenerational project entitled BRIDGES (Building Richness into the Development and Growth of Each Student) in which students adopted senior pen pals and corresponded with them regularly. Although connecting with partner teachers as well as the community takes time, McInerny found it worthwhile. When one student who is not the stereotypical "good student" is excited to share his first letter, she feels it is worth the extra time.

Perkins notes that from an academic point of view, students definitely improved their writing form and punctuation skills through the letter-writing activity. Involved in a meaningful rather than an abstract project, they were also more engaged. McInerny recognizes community service learning as a motivator for letter-writing because it revitalizes what is a rather stifling mandatory unit. Perkins notes that letter-writing is easy to learn, but tedious when not done for a real audience. She observes that students' enthusiasm and pride increases as they write to elder friends. When students acknowledge the audience receiving their correspondence, responsibility is enhanced, especially with editing and time-management skills.

Using monthly themes for their writing during BRIDGES activities, students asked their senior partners very specific questions about World War II, inventions, scientific discoveries, fashion, and music. The feedback—the real voices—elicited fascination and enthusiastic response from the youth. Many students were shocked and amazed by the experiences of the seniors, and discussion was automatically stimulated. Firsthand accounts, students felt, differed greatly from textbook coverage.

McInerny stimulated initial conversation by giving students leading questions so that the letters had a purpose. She notes that her teaching became more individualized once she started to meet with BRIDGES students. The student-teacher relationship changed, she notes, as students saw a more human side of their instructor. For Perkins, teaching focused more on affective learning than in typical instruction. Spending time on feelings and cause and effect required her to process with the students. For example, when she asked how the class might make the seniors feel more welcomed, they responded with suggestions of greeting and taking the coats of the older guests. Everyone acted as a team with a common mission to make the letter-writing a meaningful experience. Moreover, as an integral part of the planning process, the students had more choice and thus more power.

The seniors were easier to get involved once they saw how polite and nonjudgmental the kids were. The process became a reciprocal learning experience. McInerny views the project as facilitating public relations because positive attitudes were generated at all levels. The community respected the educational process, and learning became purposeful. The first year of the project fit the "show me" category for the community—but once they recognized its importance, outside agencies offered support so that the project could continue. As in other places where service learning is being woven into the fabric of the community, West Springfield recognized that, in McInerny's words, "community service learning is the way of the future."

As students involved in both projects learned new definitions of "senior citizen," their notion of this population expanded. As they watched senior tap dancers, or learned details about the lives of their partners, many responded by saying, "I didn't know senior citizens could do this." Before their contact with their senior partners, many students had a fixed notion of the older age group—for example, not recognizing significant differences between nursing home and retirement home residents. The community-service-learning experience broke down stereotypes both ways: The younger group's impression of the seniors changed, as well as the seniors' impression of the adolescents. Original reluctance to be involved often rested on these biases; but once the biases were lifted, all partners became more enthusiastic and dedicated to staying in touch. Concurrently, students became involved in the curriculum—whether history or language arts—and their enthusiasm spilled over into their schoolwork. Letter-writing and history will never be the same for these students.

11

Enhancing Peer Mediation Through Community Service Learning

Denise Messina, Mediation Coordinator,
Forest Park Middle School, Springfield, Massachusetts

Peer mediation programs are probably the most popular and widespread examples of community-service-learning programs in middle and high schools today, although they are not commonly recognized as such. Frequently, within a school system, neither technical consultants to the peer mediation programs nor the immediate school department supervisor understand the relationship between community service learning (CSL) and peer mediation. Many schools with successful peer mediation programs would not categorize their programs as community service learning. Viewing these programs as discrete entities is yet another example of effective innovations that exist in schools in isolation from one another. As we have found, however, many programs—especially community service learning and peer mediation—can enhance and support each other when staff members cooperate and coordinate with each other and the community. Community service learning can be the *main vehicle of instruction* in any discipline.

Forest Park Middle School is an urban school of approximately 900 students in grades 6–8. The school has a diverse student body.

Fleet Youth Leadership Program

As the Peer Mediation Coordinator at Forest Park Middle School in Springfield, Massachusetts, I was like most mediation coordinators—I understood community service, but I was not familiar with the philosophy and process of community service learning and was unaware of the complementary nature of the peer mediation process to community service learning. After our program had been in place for a year, however, I was considering further training and outreach ideas with several peer mediators.

At this point, our school began a business partnership with Fleet Bank. The bank, with a national and regional Youth Leadership Program based on CSL, provided CSL training—at our school—for parents and school and bank staff willing to serve as advisors to groups of students. Through this initial training, I was able to recognize that the peer mediation program was, indeed, an example of service learning. The CSL and unique Youth Leadership model that Fleet Bank presented provided the students and myself a framework to further our exploration and enhanced our motivation for community outreach activities. Fleet Bank made additional training available to us through the regional Community Service Learning Center, in collaboration with the University of Massachusetts. This training provided the insight required for us to envision the next step.

Through the training, interested parents and school and bank staff became knowledgeable and enthusiastic about CSL. We then formed 13 Fleet Youth Leadership groups of eight to nine students each. These groups met weekly with their advisors to identify, define, and problem-solve around community issues. Fleet Bank permitted employees to become co-advisors for the groups, so that each group had either a parent or teacher paired with a bank employee. This co-advisor model created interesting dynamics and relationships, unfamiliar to each of us in our traditional roles and settings. As advisors, parents, teachers, and bank employees acted as coaches or facilitators, allowing students and their ideas to take the lead, but providing resources, support, and direction when required. Bank employees were released during working hours and students and staff released during scheduled classes, with an additional activity period used for regular meetings. Community service learning in these groups was enhanced as Fleet Bank offered incentives and created opportunities to support the ongoing efforts of these 13 groups. Our partnership with Fleet Bank enabled us to experience a working model of collaboration.

The nine student mediators involved in the CSL group I advised were motivated to take their experience in violence prevention and mediation beyond their school community; and they developed their ideas and tasks. Calling themselves the Mediation Outreach Group, they worked individually, in pairs, and in small groups, sometimes requiring assistance, sometimes not. Much like subcommittees, they researched and implemented each idea, always returning to the whole group to collaborate and share. They took turns taking and recording meeting notes, taking pictures, making phone calls, writing letters, researching, and preparing for tasks. Our role as advisors was to facilitate, helping the students process and identify the next steps in their action plan and providing resources when necessary.

Accomplishments

The accomplishments of the Mediation Outreach CSL group went beyond our expectations. Our action plan evolved to include many activities, such as the following:

• In their research, group members discovered 55 youth- and family-serving agencies and centers in the community that might be interested in mediation.

• They produced a brochure to describe the mediation process and their volunteer services as mediators.

• They sought and received funding for costs to distribute the brochures to those agencies.

• They wrote letters to our Congressman, Senator, and President Clinton, expressing their views and requesting that mediation as community service be part of the National Service Trust Act.

• They developed a presentation to promote mediation as a method to curb violence and delivered it to local elementary school classes.

• They sought and received grant funding from a local cable endowment to produce an informational program on peer mediation.

• They promoted their work as mediators in addressing violence— giving various media interviews; drafting news releases; presenting at conferences, fairs, and forums; and participating on committees.

• Their work continues, recently including testimony in a public hearing before the State House Committee on Education for a House bill on violence prevention and before the State Board of Education.

Benefits and Awards

Our school, in collaboration with Fleet Bank, has instituted an annual community service fair, held in the winter, to introduce students and staff to ongoing community service and volunteer opportunities. Community needs then can be identified and explored, potentially leading to CSL integration in core curriculum. At a culminating school-wide CSL Fair, held in the spring, each group displays and shares its projects with the student body and staff.

Fleet Bank sponsored both local and state forums at which the groups each made presentations about their CSL projects to a committee that included bank and community leaders. The bank honored all the outstanding CSL groups in the state. Our group was selected as the outstanding CSL project at the local forum, and we went on to the state level to represent our school and community. We were then selected as the most outstanding CSL project in the state. Our award included a four-day trip to Washington, D.C., during which we presented our ideas on mediation to our Congressman and Senator.

Fleet Bank has continued to support the work of peer mediation in our school. This past year, we had three four-day mediation training sessions for both students and staff. Generously allowing us to use their corporate conference room for training was a strong symbol of support. In return, we offered the mediation training to bank employees.

Fleet Bank's Youth Leadership Program brought the process of service learning to life for all those involved. Knowledge of community service learning empowered the school's peer mediators to expand their scope and reach out into the neighborhood and the community to address the issue of violence.

The partnership of Forest Park Middle School and Fleet Bank is an example of an integrated business partnership and a true collaborative effort. The partnership has been mutually beneficial, both in human terms, as ongoing relationships were developed, and in public relations terms, as the students and the school were recognized for their efforts and the bank was lauded for its in-depth community involvement. The school and community overcame barriers that too frequently prevent such coordination and cooperation.

Barriers to Program Coordination

Only recently have there been opportunities for educators, especially within a system, to network, to use each other as resources and build on each other's successes and failures, and to support each other, as should occur in a community with common goals. Territorialism and possessiveness—of both materials and staff assignments—have too frequently blocked the development of networking and identification with a broader purpose and community. There is a real and legitimate explanation of why this has occurred.

In the education and human services fields, the justification of one's own position, program, and staff often becomes the overriding principle. It works against cooperation and coordination. Even at the risk of duplicating services and curriculum, people try to protect their own programs. Although a great deal of emphasis is being placed on the development of collaborative efforts through funding requirements, real collaboration is still uncommon. And peer mediation programs, although effective models of experiential learning in the school community, are not commonly identified as opportunities to further students' and schools' connection to community service learning.

Service-Learning Standards Applied to Peer Mediation

When one considers the methods and standards of service learning, as defined by the Alliance for Service Learning in Education Reform, one easily recognizes key CSL components in the implementation of a peer mediation model in a school. These components include the identification of a community problem, interdisciplinary training programs, experiential learning and assessment, and reflection (see "Standards of Quality" by the Alliance in the "Resources" section of this book).

Students who volunteer to be trained as peer mediators have identified school and community violence as a serious concern and are willing to make a serious commitment to address the issue. Students, as well as staff, feel that in addressing the resolution of student conflict in their school community, they are making a real and meaningful contribution to that community.

Peer mediators participate in an intensive training period that, ideally, is co-curricular or integrated into the academic schedule, rather than extra-curricular. It is cross-graded. The learning experiences that take place through training are experiential, engaging students in role-plays modeled on real-life situations and requiring them to use their newly acquired knowledge and communication skills. After students complete their training, they take part in authentic assessments, in which they are carefully assigned school conflict cases and monitored by the school's mediation coordinator. The period of debriefing that follows a mediation includes processing and self-evaluation and clearly corresponds to the reflection component of service learning. Incidental and related outcomes include applying these skills outside the school community, in their neighborhoods and families, as well as developing an awareness and sense of concern for the larger community. Clearly, the peer mediation model meets the standards for a CSL program.

Although an effective peer mediation program has most probably used CSL methodology, it may not be recognized as such. Responsive and perceptive mediation coordinators, sensitive to the developing interests and skills of the peer mediators, may begin to consider other learning opportunities for those students, as we did with the Fleet Youth Leadership Program.

12

Students Take the Lead in AIDS Education

Julie Coar, Student, Gig Harbor High School,
Gig Harbor, Washington

I've found that even though I'm only a seventeen-year-old high school student, people value what I'm doing. . . . What I do matters.

Gig Harbor is a small, conservative community located on Puget Sound in Washington State. The local high school, Gig Harbor High School, is one of few schools that offer a service leadership class. I was fortunate to be able to take this course during my sophomore, junior, and senior years.

I became interested in HIV/AIDS education as a result of my friend's uncle dying of AIDS and my concern that young people were not receiving the education needed to protect themselves. They don't see it now, but in 10 or 20 years *they* may be the ones testing HIV-positive. I want to prevent that from happening. I felt that our school was not doing an effective job of educating students on this subject. Although HIV is a life-threatening virus, it was never discussed in detail or addressed by people to whom the students would listen. Peer education has a greater impact for many young people because they are more open to discussing their concerns when interacting with peers. It also serves as a model, encouraging students to become involved and take action.

This chapter was written when I was a senior at Gig Harbor High School; currently, I attend the Evergreen State College in Olympia, Washington.

APEX Group

For these reasons, we formed a local chapter of the APEX group (AIDS Peer Education Exchange) and developed a peer HIV/AIDS education program. Even though this was a new approach to the state-mandated HIV/AIDS education, our teacher and principal encouraged us to explore it.

In the process, I learned about curriculum development. As a student, I was unaware of how complex a specific curriculum must be. Developing our curriculum made me more focused on the goals of each section and clear about the desired outcomes. In addition, I wanted to help create a program that was both interactive and inclusive—not boring with lectures exclusively addressing a minority of the students' needs. Our presentations became more creative and humorous . . . and one of the results was a videotaped skit we produced called "The Brady's Get Tested!"

Because we wanted more information about AIDS, I took workshops along with adults. It was interesting to listen to other's points of view. I think the adults valued hearing the youth perspective, while I found it fascinating to discover how adults viewed the issue of AIDS, and their reactions to young people's involvement in AIDS education. Unfortunately, we don't get this opportunity very often in regular classrooms. In addition, the adult workshops helped me find resources and people who could help me with my project. A healthy relationship between adults and youth is essential to a successful community project.

Learning skills such as how to run meetings and how to manage conflict became familiar and comfortable when applied to our project. We gained the needed skills to make a point coherently and to organize information into a presentation for the school board or for the state Office of Public Instruction. The whole process enhanced our communication skills as we learned to set meeting agendas, follow up with thank you's, and interact with people effectively.

We also learned to see a job through to the end. APEX members met for two or three hours in the evening once a week to gain more knowledge and plan the presentations. In 1992, we presented 100 minutes of HIV/AIDS education to small classes. Most of our presentation involved interacting with the class because our goal was to stay away from typical and ineffective preaching. Many students were inspired to see peers taking education into their hands, and our presentations empowered students to use their intellect and creativity to educate others and make significant positive improvement in their school and community.

Dealing with Community Concerns

After our first year, a small vocal group in the community asked the district to abolish the program. The school administration formed a committee consisting of teachers, students, parents, community members, and health professionals to resolve this conflict. Although these meetings were intense and sometimes hostile, we gained valuable communication skills.

Resolving this conflict required that we listen to the opposition's point of view without interrupting or making judgments. It also required that we compromise. Though I had practiced these skills in the past, it was more helpful for me to learn as I applied them to this tense situation. These meetings made positive changes in the way we presented ourselves and received other's opinions. With a great deal of help from members of the community, we presented our finished curriculum to the Office of the Superintendent of Public Instruction. This year students' parents may choose whether they are more comfortable with an APEX student educating their child or a qualified adult. Although we are disappointed that students are seen as not being competent enough to make their own choice, it is a step in the right direction.

New Student/Teacher Relationships

Our teacher is more of a mentor than an authority—a person who inspires and empowers us. He helps us to discover, and he has helped our class overcome personal doubts and strive for excellence. He broke down the wall between student and teacher, enabling us to work together. Not only does he allow us to question and explore our educational experiences, he demands it. Most important, our teacher treats us with respect—he has faith that *we are capable of accomplishing anything we set our minds to.*

I believe there's a great need for more hands-on programs in other subject areas, such as science or math. It helps me to know that I have knowledge that enables me to *do* something, not just take a test.

I'm aware that not all people learn best in this interactive approach to learning. But I know that I am more successful when I feel a sense of accountability and independence, along with support and encouragement. It is for that reason that I intend to go on to a college which also encourages this type of independent learning.

77

In retrospect, our program was possible only with the integration of service leadership into the curriculum and the continual support of our teacher and principal. The typical student/educator relationship is one of listener/lecturer. The unique structure of the service leadership class allows the students to create programs while the staff act as facilitators and supporters. All members of our group feel a deep sense of accomplishment, a feeling unique to service.

I hope that other schools will follow the lead of Gig Harbor High School and allow hands-on learning to take place through service leadership classes. Although I'm not sure what I will do for a career, I know that I enjoy working with people and that my experiences with HIV/AIDS education will have a big influence on my choices for the future.

Part IV

The School as Community Partner

13

Vision for the 21st Century: Seamless Relationship Between School and Community

Peter J. Negroni, Superintendent,
Springfield Public Schools, Springfield, Massachusetts

For the first time in this experiment called the American Democracy, educators are expected to do something never done before in the history of the world: educate everyone and educate them in such a way that they can effectively participate in an increasingly technological world. This new expectation of education for all is occurring at a most curious time in our development, when rapid demographic changes, as well as serious economic challenges, are taking up much of our energy.

Rather than feel helpless in the face of existing societal conditions, we should feel that we've been given an opportunity for action. Every educator in the United States understands that the present delivery model of education is not meeting the needs of our children and, therefore, the needs of the country. We are all struggling to understand and meet the new requirements that confront us.

It has become clear that the problem with schools is not that they *aren't* what they used to be, but that, indeed, they *are* what they used to be. Schools must change. Schools cannot continue to exist separate and apart from the rest of the community. Schools cannot continue to work in isolation, as if our work has no relationship to the larger society and the issues facing it. Schools must recognize the total interdependence of the quality of schooling and the quality of life in a community. Schools and community are totally interconnected, interwoven, and critically dependent on each other.

The community and the schools clearly must adopt common goals, values, needs, and expectations to produce individuals who care about the betterment of society. The community is everyone—adults, the young, parents, business members, social service agencies, the judicial system, and the schools—who will prepare tomorrow's contributing citizens. What occurs in the community is reflected in the schools; what occurs in the schools ultimately affects the community.

The community's responsibility to the schools includes personal involvement and financial support. Individual volunteers support the school as tutors, assistants in libraries, and chaperons on field trips and provide a consistent and caring presence for students; businesses contribute generously, not only financially but with human resources, which provide incentives for improved attendance and for academic achievement.

To understand this relationship, we must take a new look at schools and how they relate to the larger community. Educators must be at the forefront of establishing new relationships. Educators must begin to make the paradigm shifts required to make the schools a complete and total part of our community. This requires enormous change on the part of teachers and the community at large. This requires the reinvention of our schools so that they become part of the community, work for the community, and become integrated into the total community.

Change, of course, is not a simple task. Schools have existed in the United States for over 350 years with very little change. In addition, today only 23 percent of Americans have children in school. It is difficult for the remaining 77 percent to understand how critical it is that schools and community be linked if our goal is the full and effective participation of all citizens in democracy.

Community Partnerships

Springfield, Massachusetts, has tried to implement the link between the school and community by engaging the community in many new roles. Members of the Springfield community are actively participating on School-Centered Decision-Making Teams. Each team, the individual school's governing body, comprises the principal, teachers, a business representative, and parents—with an equal number of teachers and parents, depending on the size of the school. At the secondary level, students are also part of the teams. Each member has an equal voice. All decisions are reached through consensus. Through this governance structure, our school system underscores the common goals and responsibilities of the entire community to the schools.

Beyond the individual participation of businesses with the schools, the Springfield Public Schools has entered into a formal partnership with the Greater Springfield business community. Over 55 companies and the Chamber of Commerce joined in partnership with the schools to assist in common goals: reduction of the dropout rate, improved attendance, academic achievement, and development of skills for the new global economy.

Partnerships have also been formed with parents, the social service agencies, the religious community, and the legal system. Each has delineated its service and has worked with the schools to integrate a comprehensive program. Formal programs commemorated the signing of the partnerships, with the ceremonies serving as a symbol of commitment, substantive involvement, and shared responsibility for the education of our students. The partnerships are as follows:

• The Springfield Parent Advisory Network, composed of parents from each of 41 schools, was formed to address systemwide issues and to provide support to individual schools regarding their specific concerns and achievements.

• Social services are provided in the school setting. Health centers have opened in an elementary, middle, and high school. These centers treat the children on site and have decreased absenteeism.

• A Religious Initiative brought together representatives from all the religions and established a bond to work with the schools in support of education.

• The cooperative work with the police department and the court system has resulted in a model of community policing. The Student Support Team, composed of eight plainclothes police of- ficers, works in the secondary schools with the staff and students.

Community Service Learning Projects

Not only must community members and organizations go into the schools, but children must also recognize the role they can play now and later in the community. This is happening through the vehicle of community service learning projects, in which students of all ages reach out to the community to show concern and to provide assistance when and where needed.

My vision of school for the 21st century is of a totally seamless relationship between the school and the community. The school will be a place where parents, business, state and local social service agencies, not-for-profit community agencies, and the community in general interact on a daily basis; where collaborative relationships exist between and among these groups, with the school as the centerpiece of the collaboration. The school, as the focal point of the community, becomes the chief learning organization in the community; in fact, the schools become the convener of a community of learners where everyone understands that learning is both lifelong and extends beyond the school as an institution. Activities and events are integrated to engage the total larger community and the students in such a way that effective learning is taking place as a result of those relationships. School becomes a place where there is no distinction between learner and teacher.

For each person or group involved, commitment to improve the quality of life, within and without the school walls, is paramount. The school must be an integral part of the community.

14

Schools and Business Benefit Mutually Through Service Learning

Mike Bookey, President,
Digital Network Architects, Inc., Issaquah, Washington

W hen you take away all of the consequences, all you have left is irresponsibility.

Schools are modeled after the industrial factories of yesterday. The goal of the education process is to mass produce standardized, educated citizens and workers. In this factory model, we teach students the hierarchy of decision making, to follow orders, and to work individually. Businesses, however, need graduates who are self-directed, responsible employees, who can solve problems, who can handle computers and the latest technology, and who can work in teams. In this the information age, business can no longer continue to sidestep the need to reformulate the processes and goals of public education.

Electronic media and communication systems are replacing the technology of pens, pencils, paper, ink, books, trucks, autos, and airplanes as the primary means by which we record, acquire, and move information (knowledge). Today, we require information workers in business to be skilled in the use of electronic media as a condition of employment. In the future, a person not adept at working with electronic media and communication systems will be considered functionally illiterate. This is the same label we use today to describe people not able to read or write using paper and pen. Despite this remarkable transformation to electronic technology in society, our public schools continue to function as if nothing has changed. The last stronghold of paper technology and the industrial process is our public schools. It is ironic that an institution specifically charged with preparing our young people for the future, so fervently clings to the past.

One way business can help is to work with schools to provide opportunities for students to participate in meaningful situations in their schools and communities, outside the four walls of a classroom. Business/school partnerships have traditionally been viewed as a way for business to help schools assist needy students. Businesses have provided tutoring, materials, and funding for field trips. Though these are valuable resources, businesses can play a more vital role in restructuring the educational process by working with schools to develop opportunities for young people to participate in the functioning of their school and community.

Technology Information Project

Through the Technology Information Project (TIP) in the Issaquah School District in Washington State, young people have played a central role in bringing technology into their schools and community. Succeeding generations of students have built and now operate a computer network of more than 2,000 computers encompassing 20 school locations. Every classroom and office computer connects to a school local area network (LAN). Each school LAN links to a wide area network, creating a District Enterprise network. The District Enterprise network connects to the Internet. The Internet connection enables parents, teachers, students, and local businesses to send e-mail to one another; it allows students to access knowledge bases throughout the world; and it enables teachers to electronically communicate with parents about their children's progress. Students are now working to build an Internet Web service that will provide their community with information about Issaquah Schools, city government, city police and fire departments, local community groups, and instructional resources for home schooling.

Students and teachers at Issaquah have worked together to develop the TIP network. DNA's role was to provide technical assistance to this process, but teachers and students were the ones who made it happen. Many schools are encouraging teachers to get away from the traditional "teacher-as-lecturer" role and move to the role of coach, giving students the opportunity to be on the playing field. If business is to be provided with a team of talented players, business leaders must also take on the role of coach and help create opportunities for students to develop their skills on "real-life" playing fields. Businesses can expand the playing field by offering students and teachers expert knowledge of computer and communication technology. A number of examples are currently taking place in the state of Washington.

Students' Projects

Students Develop Products.

• In Tacoma, Washington, a hospital physical therapist sent a videotape of an 18-month-old child with multiple sclerosis to a high school Industrial Design class. The students built a wheelchair that was mobile and had the capacity to be enlarged as the child grew. Students applied technical knowledge and problem-solving skills to this project and were rewarded with a feeling of great joy as they saw the smiles of gratitude from this child and his parents.

• MicroSoft puts students to work as part-time managers. They work with software developers to write codes, work in test teams to debug them, and send their work back to developers and then to Release Coordinators and marketing people. Schools have been used by MicroSoft as Beta Test sites for a number of networking systems. Several students now run a consulting business to help schools and small businesses set up computer networks.

Students Do Research.

• The Tree Top company has involved students in research on certain fungi that affect the fruit crop. In exchange, the company provides the science class with the latest technology. Because they know that their research will actually affect the local economy and local farming practices, students have a strong commitment to quality control; and students' research benefits the community.

• The U.S. Environmental Protection Agency (EPA) has partnered with a number of school districts, funding students' data collection on significant environmental issues, such as wetlands preservation and air particulates. Students in the science classes begin to connect their chemistry and biology studies and apply them to a local environmental issue. At the same time, EPA has exponentially expanded its "work force," collecting more valuable data for policy making and engendering an ethic of environmental stewardship.

Students Develop Marketing or Community Outreach Programs.

Seattle City Light contracted with a high school drama department to develop districtwide energy conservation assemblies. Students were involved in all phases of the program, from dramatics, lighting, and design to performance management; and they produced a top-quality program. Evaluations indicated the these assemblies were more engaging than were previous programs because the high school students had a natural rapport with the elementary audience and were willing to take risks.

Mutual Benefits

School/business partnerships work for mutual benefits in the following ways:

• Businesses can help restructure schools by updating their technology and bringing them into the "Communication Age."

• Businesses can provide opportunities for youth to apply their learning to real life, so the youth can see themselves as capable resources for their schools, businesses, and their community.

• Businesses will be provided with graduates who will be skilled, thinking, capable employees.

15

Schools and Community-Based Organizations: Partnerships Based on History

Rick Jackson, Vice President, YMCA of Greater Seattle,
Seattle, Washington

During the early 1900s, when young people were no longer needed as a part of the rural farm economy, community-based youth organizations such as YMCAs/YWCAs, Campfire, Scouts, 4–H, and Boys and Girls Clubs were developed to provide positive ways to engage young people in their communities. Communities recognized that they needed new ways to provide meaningful roles for youth that would provide character and leadership development.

Changes in society in recent years have caused many community youth groups to change their focus. Women have moved from the home to the workplace, and many organizations have lost their traditional leaders—such as Cub Scout den mothers and leaders of Campfire groups. In addition, many of these programs have been forced to change their focus from involving young people in positive youth activities to providing social services like counseling, youth employment, gang interventions, and alternative education programs.

Educators are concerned by this change in focus. Although they see the need for direct services, they feel that positive youth development should involve kids in fun, fellowship, and service, the core values of many youth-serving organizations. This would eliminate much of the need for youth intervention and remediation. If youth have positive things to do, including good relations with peers, access to mentors and role models, and worthwhile group experiences, their values and character will develop naturally.

Community-based organizations can be wonderful partners for school-based youth service because the development of youth-group programs have these principles at their roots:

- Experiential learning
- Youth-group workers as built-in role models
- Community involvement as an essential part of program development

It is for these reasons that community-based community service can become a powerful partner of the schools. The YMCA Earth Service Corps program, for instance, which involves many schools and communities, teaches leadership skills and the ethic of environmental involvement. For many youth, YMCAs are a more effective learning setting than the school simply because *they aren't school*.

As we move to the concept of "learning communities," as schools become more connected to the community, as an increasing number of community-based organizations reach out to work with a broader base of youth, and as schools operate with ever-decreasing funding, schools will begin to operate as *brokers of varied education options*. These types of partnerships will better service youth in their personal, social, and academic development.

16

Youth Corps Makes Middle School Connection

Ira Harkavy, Director, Center for Community Partnerships,
Assistant to the President, University of Pennsylvania,
Philadelphia, Pennsylvania

Cory Bowman, Assistant Director, Penn Program for Public Service,
University of Pennsylvania, Philadelphia, Pennsylvania

The West Philadelphia Improvement Corps (WEPIC) is a school-based school and community revitalization project founded in 1985. WEPIC seeks to create comprehensive community schools that are the social, service delivery, and educational hubs for the entire community.

West Philadelphia Improvement Corps

WEPIC's goal is to produce comprehensive community schools that serve, educate, involve, and activate all members of the community. Ultimately, the Corps intends to help develop schools that are open to the public 24 hours a day, 365 days a year, functioning simultaneously as the core building for the community and as the educational and service delivery hub for students, their families, and other local residents. WEPIC originated in the spring of 1985 from an honors history seminar on "Urban Universities-Community Relationships: Penn-West Philadelphia, Past, Present and Future, as a Case Study," co-taught by University of Pennsylvania President Sheldon Hackney and historians Lee Benson and Ira Harkavy. Undergraduate students in that seminar focused their research on different problems in the West Philadelphia community.

Though WEPIC began as a youth corps program, it is currently a year-round program involving more than 2,000 children, their parents, and community members in education and cultural programs, recreation, job training, and community improvement and service activities. It is coordinated by the West Philadelphia Partnership—a mediating, nonprofit, community-based organization composed of institutions (including the University of Pennsylvania)—and community groups, in conjunction with the Greater Philadelphia Urban Affairs Coalition and the Philadelphia School District. Other partners in the effort include unions; job training agencies; churches; community groups; and city, state, and federal agencies and departments.

The academic work done with the WEPIC Schools is based on a community-oriented, real-world, problem-solving approach; activities are focused on areas chosen by each school's principal and staff. In this neo-Deweyan approach, students not only learn by doing, but also learn by and for service.

The university and other community partners provide the resources that make each of the WEPIC School programs possible. WEPIC is assisted by the University of Pennsylvania (Penn), VISTA Volunteers, local health institutions including Misericordia Hospital, the Penn Medical Center, Greater Philadelphia Health Action, and other community agencies and services.

Dr. John P. Turner Middle School

Though WEPIC works with more than 14 schools, the major site has been the Dr. John P. Turner Middle School—a majority African American school with a sizable percentage of students from families that live below the poverty level. The components of the Turner/WEPIC School include the school-day health-based House (or school-within-a-school), after-school programs, Saturday Morning and Wednesday Evening Schools, a Summer Institute, various parent-involvement and University and community volunteer programs, a social health program, and WEPIC expansion and replication activities.

The overarching theme of the in-school House is community health, around which a new community-service-learning curriculum is being developed and implemented on an ongoing basis with the assistance of the University of Pennsylvania Graduate School of Education.

The House's goal is not only to improve students' basic skills and abilities to make healthy decisions, but also to help students become agents for change in their community and to be educators of their peers, family, and community members. The House's central projects are service-learning activities, including peer education, community outreach, and work-based learning. These activities are integrating and motivating vehicles for the WEPIC curriculum, which uses community-oriented, project-based, team-taught, interdisciplinary units to teach academic and personal growth skills. Community service learning—its preparation, service activities, and reflection—is integrated with the basic content areas of math, science, social studies, and language arts. Community service learning and the school district's curriculum reinforce each other and are enhanced by their implementation through WEPIC's team-teaching, project-oriented approach.

Student Projects

Career exposure, work-based learning, and peer teaching activities are linked to the curriculum. For example, students keep journals about their experiences and they interview and observe health care professionals at different levels and jobs, learning about health care delivery and training. In class, students make formal presentations and participate in group discussions based on their journals.

All 6th grade students participate in a nutrition education program, generally aided and also taught twice a week by students in Penn's Anthropology Department. Students learn about healthy nutrition habits, basic science relating to nutrition, and reading food labels. The department is working with the staff to create a nutrition curriculum for Turner that will be desktop published. This nutrition education program serves as the foundation for the students' future peer and community outreach projects. Some of these projects are as follows:

• About 10 students in each 7th grade section (a total of 40 students) participate in a peer-teaching project at Turner's three feeder elementary schools. Turner students build on their 6th grade learning and teach the elementary students about basic nutrition and healthy habits.

• All 7th grade students learn about a community health topic each quarter and then host a Community Health Watch at Turner. Topics have included hypertension, nutrition, injury prevention awareness and home screening, cancer (breast, lung, and colon) detection and screening, HIV/AIDS education and screening, and drug and alcohol abuse.

Students learn about the definitions, causes, risk factors, community prevalence, treatment, and preventive measures and healthy decisions relating to a particular topic. They present that information in the classroom and community forums.

• All grades participate in a community history project and in career-exposure programs that provide guest speakers and field trips.

• While the students educate their peers, family, and community members about healthy decisions and habits, WEPIC coordinates appropriate student and adult screenings and makes available professional advice relating to the Health Watch Theme. Services have included free, anonymous HIV screening during the AIDS/HIV Health Watch and free breast cancer screenings and mammography vouchers during Cancer Health Watch.

• A student from Penn's Graduate School of Education works with House staff (primarily 7th grade) as a health resources and curriculum coordinator. An Assistant Professor of Medicine at Penn coordinates the efforts of the Penn Medical Center in staffing and providing technical assistance for Community Health Watch lectures and demonstrations, cultivates job-training sites at Penn's Medical Center, helps staff the Community Health Watch screenings, and serves as a resource for the development of Turner's health curriculums.

• About 10 students from each 8th grade section (a total of 40 students) will participate in a work-based learning project at local health care institutions, Misericordia, Woodland Avenue Heath Center, and the Hospital of the University of Pennsylvania. Some of these students will participate in the West Philadelphia High School/*Philadelphia Tribune* (Philadelphia's largest African American newspaper) desktop-publishing program.

• Students in the allied health careers project rotate through various departments of a hospital (e.g., dietary, nursing, respiratory, community outreach, patient representative, and hospital administration), are assigned individual hospital-based mentors, and participate in discussions related to the education and training required for various hospital personnel.

Role of the Partners

The University of Pennsylvania plays a significant support role in all WEPIC activities at Turner. An ongoing project of the Graduate School of Education is to work closely with teachers to develop thematic, integrated curriculums. The Anthropology Department teaches 6th graders nutrition and prepares them to be peer educators; this department also is working with the Turner staff to create a service-learning-oriented nutrition textbook. The Penn Medical Center plays a leading role in providing work-based learning experience. Other Penn schools with significant programs at Turner include Arts and Sciences, Law, Dental, Medical, and Nursing.

The partnership has fostered other school-community partnerships that involve business and health care providers. WEPIC now has several replication activities underway that focus on University-Community School partnerships, including a national replication grant from DeWitt Wallace-Readers' Digest Fund and a local replication grant from the Corporation on National and Community Service.

Part V

Reflection

17

Reflection as a Tool for Turning Service Experiences into Learning Experiences

James Toole and Pamela Toole, Co-Directors,
Compass Institute, St. Paul, Minnesota

The salvation of this human world lies nowhere else than in the human heart, in the human power to reflect, in human meekness and in human responsibility.
— Czechoslovakian President Vaclav Havel,
addressing the U.S. Congress (February 1990)

It is good that many schools nowadays can provide a rich and interesting environment for their pupils, especially in the early stages of their schooling. . . . The problem is, we are often so busy in-putting, that adequate time (let alone ample) is rarely offered to children to rediscover what has "sunk in," in order to reflect on it further before they are required to re-present what they have "learned."
— Pat D'Arcy (1989)
in *Making Sense, Shaping Meaning*

Community-service-learning projects are potentially wonderful "textbooks." They involve complex problems, real-life contexts, and exposure to people who possess wide expertise and resources not found in schools. Both the challenge and the strength of such textbooks is that they come without chapters, footnotes, labeled pictures, list of key concepts, and review questions at the end. If students are going to learn from service, it will not be instant or effortless. They will be required to organize and construct their own understanding from the rich content embedded within these experiences.

For this reason, no activity is more central to understanding and implementing service-learning programs than reflection. In a frequently cited passage, Dan Conrad and Diane Hedin (1987, p. 39) point out:

> To say that experience is a good teacher . . . does not imply that it's easily or automatically so. If it were, we'd all be a lot wiser than we are. It's true that we can learn from experience. We may also learn nothing. Or we may, like Mark Twain's cat who learned from sitting on a hot stove lid never to sit again, learn the wrong lesson.

In service learning, the term *reflection* refers to those thinking processes responsible for converting service experiences into productive learning experiences.

Our most persistent observation from several years of intensive staff development work in this field, however, is that the connections between service projects and formal learner outcomes are often underdeveloped. Although service-learning practitioners give universal homage to the term *reflection*, it is rarely, if ever, defined or well understood. Teachers, who are responsible for helping students to link service and learning, frequently lament: "Reflection. That's the part that I have not been doing very well."

In this chapter, we suggest a definition of reflection for the field of service learning, describe how it might look and operate within a classroom, and present a variety of practical strategies that teachers can use.

Reflection Defined

When people reflect in everyday life, they pause to review, ponder, contemplate, analyze, or evaluate an experience or information to gain deeper understanding. This ability to reflect gives people the freedom, power, and responsibility, perhaps unique among all living things, to continually choose or adjust the direction of their lives. That is why reflection is at the heart of becoming a self-directed and lifelong learner. For the purposes of applying this concept to service learning, we define reflection as the *use of creative and critical thinking skills to help prepare for, succeed in, and learn from the service experience, and to examine the larger picture and context in which the service occurs.* Let's look closer at some of the words used in the definition:

1. *Critical Thinking Skills.* If students are to do more than simply recount their service experience, teachers must challenge and teach their pupils how to think critically—to make observations and inferences, to analyze a situation, to organize and interpret information, to weigh the accuracy of diverse points of view, to develop and defend their solutions, and to evaluate the results and assess the meaning of their work. Because learning and practicing these skills improve the quality and output of student dialogue, such practice should form the cornerstone for reflective sessions. To think reflectively is to think critically.

2. *Creative Thinking Skills.* We have included creative as well as critical thinking because we reflect not only to understand, but also to create—to generate as well as to evaluate. Creativity is central to the mission of service learning because there are few community problems that are not in great need of fresh thinking, ingenuity, and imagination. Involvement in service can provide students with an internship in how to develop innovative solutions to address important community needs, such as the following:

- At a South Central Los Angeles high school, students raise and market "Food From the 'Hood" (including a natural foods salad dressing called "Straight Out the Garden") to raise money to rebuild their community and fund college scholarships.

- On an Evergreen, Washington, middle school campus, an entire student body voted to build and operate the area's first native plant wetland nursery to restore local stream beds.

- In rural Minnesota, a 3rd grade class, to renovate their city's neglected rest stop on the state highway, prepared a plan, secured governmental approval, raised resources, and completed the painting and landscaping required to give the place new life.

3. *Reflection as a "Help."* Reflection plays a vital but not exclusive role in the educational dimension of service-learning projects. When students tackle community problems, they not only need to reflect; they must often learn new skills and knowledge. To prepare for a service project, for instance, students may need instruction in how to conduct interviews, lobby state legislators, care for injured wildlife, conduct water-quality testing, or take someone's blood pressure—all of which might be taught through direct instruction.

4. *Preparing, Succeeding, and Learning.* Although the literal definition of reflection means "looking backward," reflection occurs at every

phase of the service-learning cycle: reflection to prepare for service, reflection during action, and reflection upon action. The idea is that thoughtfulness permeates the entire service endeavor. Reflection plays a distinct role at each stage. In one cross-age tutoring program, for example, the preparation of the older students included reflecting about what they were like at the same age as their tutees. During the project, students reflected on the frustrations and problems they were encountering as tutors and brainstormed solutions. Finally, after the project, students reflected to synthesize what they had learned about teaching, about helping others, and about themselves.

5. *Examine the Larger Picture.* Too often, people limit the focus of reflection to affective issues ("How did you feel about the project?") or only to the service project itself. The potential educational outcomes increase dramatically when teachers and students connect the service experience to broader, more comprehensive themes.

If students are volunteering at a hospital, for example, the same experience might be used to support outcomes in youth development, citizenship, vocational education, or any academic subject. It depends on which lens the students and teacher place over the experience. If the focus is on vocational education, students might select a career to investigate. From a civic education point of view, students could examine the issue of health care reform through research and interviews with medical staff, or debate the justice and feasibility of universal health care. In terms of personal development, a teacher might ask students to write about how the helping experience or the exposure to those who are ill has changed them. Academically, a hospital can offer an opportunity to learn science, math, health education, communication, artistic design, and even foreign languages.

Envisioning Reflective Classrooms

Service learning stretches the typical classroom format. When students act as health peer educators, museum guides, hospital volunteers, or conflict mediators, they enter situations that, like all real-life contexts, are full of unpredictability, novelty, and the need for quick decision making. Students are required not only to recall information, but to apply it using insight, judgment, know-how, and even wisdom. They therefore require a classroom that gives them the intellectual elbow room to pose their own problems, face perplexity, hypothesize, organize and interpret experience, and search for meaning.

Donald Schon (1983, 1987), whose landmark work has been directed at improving professional education in the United States, has written extensively about one model of such a classroom that he calls a "reflective practicum." It is an intriguing mixture of terms because reflective typically means to stand back from the world, and practicum means to be immersed in it. It is a model already found in studios of art and design, conservatories of music and dance, athletics, counseling, and apprenticeships in the crafts. The defining characteristic of all of these learning environments is that students are required to *demonstrate* some competency—either to perform a skill or create a genuine product. Because one can't learn to play the violin or professionally counsel someone solely from textbooks or lectures, such classrooms require a combination of real-life practice, traditional academics, and a healthy amount of student dialogue, reflection, and self-assessment. The concept offers a perfect classroom model for service learning.

If we walked into a reflective session for service learning, students would be elaborating, questioning, and critiquing the peaks and valleys of their respective experiences from the past week. Student dialogue would be at the core of this part of the instructional process. When students brought up problems encountered in their service work, the teacher would likely turn to the group and ask, *"What do the rest of you think?"* This is what we call "biting your tongue" teaching because instructors have to be willing to avoid the tendency to give too much information and to do too much thinking for students. Here, teachers are in the role of coaches or facilitators, not "experts," because the focus is on students developing their own ability to reason and make wise decisions. Different student outcomes require different approaches to teaching (Joyce, Weil, and Showers 1992).

At first glance, this process may not seem unique. Teachers often encourage students to reflect about what they are learning. What is distinctive to service learning is that reflection is grounded in real-life roles, contexts, and performances. When elementary school students reflect on how a local stream might be restored to life, the discussion is extra lively because the class is going to evaluate and actually use the best ideas. In an art class studying pottery, students have extended conversations about the suitability of various glazes because the pottery will be used as part of an "empty bowl" luncheon project to raise money for famine relief in Africa. When middle school students take their training in first aid, they ask questions throughout because they are going to volunteer as members of a search-and-rescue team in a federal wilderness area. Necessity is not only the mother of invention; it is also the mother of significant cognition.

103

The Service-Learning Spiral

To illustrate the role of reflection within the life of a single service project, we've adapted David Kolb's (1984) model of experiential learning to show the service-learning cycle (see Figure 17.1). Our version of the model differs from others for three reasons:

1. Reflection infuses all parts of the process rather than being a stage that follows experience.

2. The cycle is shown as a spiral rather than a circle, illustrating that students bring new competence to each successive experience.

3. Although it is common and appropriate for many experiential learning activities to start with the experience itself, service-learning activities typically begin by identifying a need, creating a project to meet that need, and then planning and preparing for implementation.

FIGURE 17.1
Service-Learning Cycle

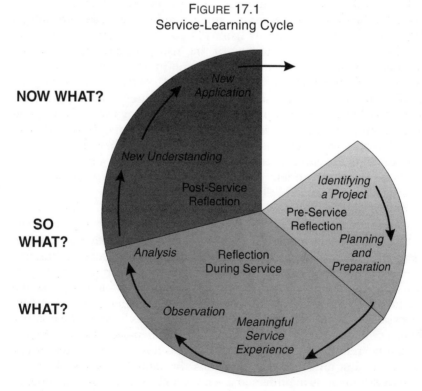

How classes identify and implement these service projects will directly affect the quality of group reflection throughout the cycle. What activates, vitalizes, and drives student thoughtfulness and dialogue is that (1) the project addresses a genuine community need—it is worthy of reflection and (2) there is some significant level of student responsibility, ownership, or choice—the outcomes are important to and in the hands of youth. Without these two attributes, even the most highly skilled adult facilitator will likely face an uncommunicative class.

In this section, we present a brief look at how reflection might contribute to each stage of the service spiral. The content before, during, and after the project can include at least three dimensions: reflection on the task itself; reflection on the social, political, economic, vocational or other contexts of the task; and reflection on related issues of the human spirit, such as questions of purpose, meaning, suffering, hope, friendship, justice, care, and responsibility.

Reflection Before Service

Reflection *before* service may seem a contradiction, but we commonly reflect on and use prior knowledge and experience when we plan and design any project. In preparing for service work, students recollect, propose, hypothesize, build models, predict and make judgments. Students reflect when they choose a service project (*What do we wish were different in our community?*); when they clarify project goals and action plans (*What do we want to see happen?*); and when they prepare for the service itself (*How do we feel about participating in this project?*). In preparing students for an intergenerational project, for instance, students might simulate and reflect on the challenges experienced by some senior citizens by sitting in a wheelchair, putting Vaseline on their glasses, and wearing thick gloves to perform fine motor tasks.

A critical component of preservice reflection involves students' examining the existence and source of their current attitudes and beliefs about immigrants, people with disabilities, the environment, or any other issue they face. Students often bring to projects preexisting ideas based on brief experiences, secondhand knowledge, or societal stereotypes. D'Arcy (1989, p. 3) cites a core principle learned from science educators in the United Kingdom: "If a pupil's own picture of how the world works is ignored, her ability to make sense of someone else's picture, the teacher's or the textbook writer's, [*or in our case, the service experience*] is seriously impeded."

A simple activity to tap existing attitudes, developed by Francis E. Pratt (n.d.) for intergenerational learning, recommends the following three-step activity:

1. List 10 words you would use to describe senior citizens (or any other group).

2. Put a plus, minus, or zero next to each trait to mark whether it is positive, negative, or neutral.

3. Write a paragraph about what you think your list reveals about your attitudes. These papers can be collected and saved, and at the end of the project, students can repeat the activity and compare the results.

At an even deeper level, Mezirow (1990) and others reserve the term *critical reflection* to refer to the examination of the often invisible premises or presuppositions that underlie our thinking. In service learning, such assumptions can help shape or determine how staff and students perceive a potential service site, frame a problem, suggest solutions, and evaluate the results. For instance, many schools initially designed projects for their students to provide help and friendship for their classmates with disabilities. After reflecting on the real purpose underneath such efforts—such as the development of interpersonal skills, self-esteem, and increased inclusion for those with disabilities— many teachers have also enlisted special needs students themselves to be in the role of helping others. In one such project, youth with Down syndrome have become caregivers to senior citizens in a convalescent home.

Reflection During Service

Although preparation is critical, it is important to remember that what really ignites student curiosity is the service work itself. The most teachable moments will arise *during* and *after* students' involvement in real-life tasks. As the 1950s Pittsburgh Pirates baseball player Vernon Law put it, *"Experience is a hard teacher because she gives the test first, the lesson after."* The practicum will offer a structured opportunity for students to assess the complex issues arising from their fieldwork. Students will report about these experiences (the "what" stage) and analyze them (the "so what" stage) using such thinking skills as recalling, observing, inferring, and classifying.

During the service project, a reflective practicum serves multiple purposes, including offering students the opportunity to share observations and highlights, ask questions, solve problems, solicit feedback, gather encouragement, and learn from classmates. For the teacher, it is an opportunity to monitor, appreciate, and supervise student work.

Reflection After Service

As Conrad and Hedin (1987) point out, experience is not the same thing as knowledge. Students can store experiences in "episodic memory" (Tulving 1983), where they can report but may not yet understand a sequence of events. In the aftermath of a project, students therefore need to formally reflect in order to evaluate the project, assess their own development, look for generalizations to guide future decision making, and find "new applications" for what they have learned. Students ask important questions:

> *What difference have we really made?*
> *What have I learned?*
> *Where might I apply this new knowledge elsewhere in my life?*
> *How has my model of the world changed and what does that mean for my life?*
> *What have I learned about myself, about those I served, and about academic skills and content?*

The answers to these questions will increase the likelihood that students will develop self-knowledge and knowledge about the world that will transfer to new situations.

Such discussions not only make educational sense in service learning; they are also an ethical requirement. If teachers are going to place students in service settings that are morally complex and challenging, they have a responsibility to provide adequate opportunities for students to discuss, make sense of, and resolve these experiences. Examples of specific strategies to help students achieve a final synthesis or closure to their learning follow in the next section.

Classroom Strategies for Reflection

In Chinese the verb *xie* is used interchangeably to describe either the act of creating a painting or a work of calligraphy. For us, this points to a wider truth. When students have something to reflect on and express, they can "write" through a journal, a poem, a drawing, a cartoon, a slide show, a short story, a speech, a dance, a song, or even a mime. These different forms of "writing," of constructing and representing meaning, are what Elliott Eisner (1991) calls *multiple forms of literacy*.

The concept of multiple forms of literacy has major implications for *how* students reflect in service-learning practicums. The person who is less comfortable in small-group discussion may make a wonderful video documenting his community garden project for the food bank. The person who can't quite find the right words to write in her journal may draw a series of political cartoons that forcefully capture her experiences in a homeless shelter. Such an approach encourages an atmosphere of creativity, comfort, and excellence among students because it affirms their particular strengths and varied intelligences (Gardner 1983). Moreover, the instructional power of all forms of representation is that they make thinking visible. All students find it possible both to share with others and to edit and refine their thinking.

In this section, we describe some of the multiple forms of literacies that students might use to reflect and represent knowledge. These strategies are not meant to be alternatives to one another. Some of the best reflective projects may include two or three different forms, such as writing and art projects or reading and class discussion. Moreover, as Harry Silcox (1993) points out, the form of reflection should be carefully chosen because it helps dictate the type of thinking and outcomes that will occur.

Writing to Reflect

When students write, they often simply "give evidence" that they can recall what the teacher taught. In contrast, service learning uses writing as a tool to produce, not reproduce, knowledge. Students fill what are variously called learning logs, reflection logs, or thinking logs, with the constructive interplay between the core classroom content and their own personal reflections.

Students can be taught to be more versatile in the number of ways that they process and record their thinking in such a notebook. Teacher "prompts" can encourage different types of critical thinking and different forms of expression, such as the following:

- Write a letter to yourself before your service work begins. What do you predict that this experience will be like for you? (*Forecasting*).

- Draw a web showing what you already know about the topic of endangered species, and what you would like to know. (*Recalling and organizing*).

- Create a flowchart to represent the steps involved in implementing your service project. (*Sequencing*).

- Write about a critical incident that happened at your site where you didn't know what to do. How did you handle it? What would you change if this happened again? (*Problem-solving*).

- Draw a diagram showing your before-and-after image of the people with whom you have been working. (*Compare and contrast*).

- If you were given the authority, how would you change how your service placement uses volunteers? (*Evaluation*).

- Where and how might you use the knowledge that you have learned from your service project? (*Application*).

- What has your service work taught you about the type of career that you would like to have or not have? (*Application*).

- Draw a cartoon that teaches something important about the people whom you are serving. (*Synthesis and creative thinking*).

Besides learning logs, service-learning projects are filled with opportunities for authentic writing products that encourage reflection and fit perfectly with a meaning-centered language arts curriculum, as the following examples illustrate:

• One kindergarten class culminated their year by creating a Big Book for each of the local nursery schools that told "the real story" about kindergarten.

• An intergenerational choir of senior citizens and fifth graders became pen pals for several months before rehearsing together.

• Middle school students volunteering in a children's science museum created their own exhibit on composting and wrote the text for the various displays.

• High school peer helpers welcoming immigrant students wrote their own "Student Handbook" and translated it into several languages.

In each of these examples, the "product" is not only a vehicle for reflection and closure; it is also a highly engaging writing task that fulfills an essential purpose by addressing and affecting a real audience.

Reading and Reflecting on the Larger Contexts of Service

In discussing the education of medical doctors, Ilene Harris (1993, p. 33) poses the question, "While knowing-in-action and reflection-in-action are essential in professional practice, what informs reflection?" Students who are highly enthusiastic about working in a homeless shelter or food bank, for instance, might *appear* to be receiving a real-life education in social studies and civic education. If what informs reflection is only the service experience itself, however, then students will not have the background to "see" or understand how to address the myriad social, political, and economic forces that converge in that experience. What students observe at a service site rarely conveys the whole story.

When students do research the wider context of their work, they develop an informed perspective that improves both the learning and the service. The students volunteering in a shelter, for example, could study interdisciplinary content in economics, political science, sociology, and psychology relevant to their work. Such background research and readings might include the social and political origins of the problem, how previous and current public policy has succeeded or failed to address the issue, and how the concepts of citizenship and social justice apply to the situation. All such work reinforces Resnick and Klopfer's (1989, p. 6) conclusion: "There is no choice to be made between a content emphasis and a thinking-skill emphasis. No depth in either is possible without the other."

One California middle school blended thinking and content through combining direct service in a shelter with a year-long original research project into specific issues about the local homeless population. The research culminated in a set of recommendations presented in a public forum to a U.S. Congressman, the head of a Stanford University Study research team, and a principal from a public school serving homeless children. These young adolescents had learned and practiced the requisite skills for influencing social policy, such as how to analyze a community problem, how to network with other organizations, and how to heighten public awareness. There was a direct and vigorous connection between the character of the students' education and their present and future role as democratic citizens.

If students in a language arts or interdisciplinary class volunteered in the same setting, they could extend their reflection through readings such as *Oliver Twist, Grapes of Wrath,* and *The Autobiography of Malcolm X.* Some of the class would likely be having volunteer experiences that could have stepped off the pages of Dickens, Steinbeck, or Malcolm X. These books have the potential to deepen the insights of students by their portrayal of the personal history, motives, complexity, strengths, frailties, and larger historical conditions of their characters' lives. In English classes, discussion would focus on the literary merit of the books and on the understanding that the authors shed on poverty both for the students' own community and as an ongoing historical issue.

In the tradition of outdoor education, readings in service learning can also take the role of inspirational quotes about concepts such as courage, persistence, integrity, leadership, or success. We may read a "quote of the day" and ask students, *"How do these apply to our immediate service work, and in our larger lives?"*

Class Discussion

Group discussion offers one powerful attribute missing in solitary reflective techniques—the opportunity to learn directly from one's peers. Cognition becomes a social process. We become excited when we hear other people give language to what we intuitively know, and we are challenged when their views differ markedly from our own. The frequent result is that the sum total of the "group wisdom" goes far beyond what our own thinking could produce.

Such dialogue, however, rarely happens automatically. It is challenging for students to think out loud and push the boundaries of their thinking in front of a group of their peers. Teachers need to give a high priority to building a shared sense of community, helping students learn group skills, and using a variety of approaches. One 3rd grade teacher who had difficulty persuading her students to discuss their work had great success when she set up a "talk show," where one student was the master of ceremonies and three students were interviewed.

If students are to expand their ability to perceive and understand the world through group dialogue, the practicum participants need to be as diverse as possible. Students will learn that their peers from different neighborhoods, social groups, and cultural backgrounds often differ in how they define problems, pay attention to certain issues, and interpret the same set of facts. Beyond this, students may also discover that these diverse points of view can be a resource when trying to understand and solve a community problem.

The Arts

Teachers might offer students a chance to document a service experience through less conventional modes such as poetry, music, cartooning, posters, videos, dance, sculpture, or photography. Dan Conrad (personal communication, July 1993), who teaches a high school service elective class in Hopkins, Minnesota, tells the story of three boys who made light of the practicum meetings and resisted all urging to write about their project. As a culmination to their volunteering at a nursing home, however, they prepared a video that captured a sensitivity and depth of understanding that they might never have been able to convey and affirm in any other form of representation.

The arts can be used to reflect throughout the service-learning cycle. To help select a service project, we have asked middle school students to draw two pictures: one of what they like and another of what they don't like about their neighborhoods. We then place the two sets of pictures on two separate walls, ask for student observations, and discuss the neighborhood's strengths and needs that are evident in the drawings. In preparing for another service project, this time with senior citizens, we have asked students to draw and share important memories from their own childhood, and then talk about the role that reminiscing and oral histories play in all of our lives.

Portfolios

Portfolios provide a structure for collecting in one place a set of records documenting the progress of a student project. Students can select a compilation of artifacts that are produced throughout the activity, such as initial plans, revisions, letters written and received, charts, artwork, journal entries, newspaper clippings, and evaluation forms. This record can be used as an ongoing vehicle for student reflection and self-assessment, for evidence of student achievement, and for sharing the service project with interested audiences. One of those audiences could be parents, as more and more school districts adopt the practice of student-led parent conferences.

Self-Assessment and Peer Assessment

A central goal of education is for students to become self-directed, lifelong learners. To achieve this goal, they must learn how to reflect, evaluate, and make judgments about their own work. One reflective technique is to ask pairs of students to meet regularly to share and assess their own progress. If students have developed a clear plan and a rubric of standards, they can use these criteria to explore their successes and determine what they need to do differently. The role of the peer assessor is to listen and ask clarifying questions, not to give grades or judgments.

Building a Reflective Future

Havel's quotation at the start of this chapter is striking because he includes "the human power to reflect" as one of four cornerstones for the world's salvation. Adult educators in our workshops nearly always agree that reflection plays a vital role in their lives, although they have to squeeze it into their days while driving a car, jogging, cleaning the house, gardening, or walking the dog. It is an ongoing struggle for most of us not only to live life, but to monitor whether we are going where we want, using the best means to get there, and discovering what it all means. Clearly this is in our individual and collective self-interest. Gaining perspective and understanding are daily needs.

Young people face an environment both in and out of school that rarely supports reflection. As Michael Oakeshott (quoted in Fuller 1989) notes in *The Voice of Liberal Learning*, our world is full of "seductive trivialities which invoke neither reflection nor choice but instant participation." We therefore need to create in our homes, schools, and community organizations the opportunity for youth to develop those attitudes and habits that produce depth, meaning, and lifelong learning. In a culture that fosters impulsiveness and offers constant entertainment, the challenge for parents and teachers is to design alternative settings that value and reward qualities like self-initiative, sustained curiosity, thoroughness, self-discipline, empathy, intellectual integrity, and ethical reasoning.

In classrooms that combine authentic tasks and reflective thinking, such habits can be reinforced; and students will have the time to extend and refine comprehension. They can practice the skills and dispositions—*the process*—of reflection to make sense of and thoughtfully guide their educational work. After years of adding to our curriculum in schools, we are coming to realize that we may not be teaching anything if students are not given the opportunity to acquire deep understanding and the ability to use what we teach. Through the effective use of service-learning programs, students can regain a greater educational locus of control to learn both content, skills and, in the words of Albert Einstein, "the courage to take your own thoughts seriously."

References

Conrad, D., and D. Hedin. (1987). *Youth Service: A Guidebook for Developing and Operating Effective Programs*. Washington, D.C.: Independent Sector.

D'Arcy, P. (1989). *Making Sense, Shaping Meaning*. Portsmouth, N.H.: Heinemann.

Eisner, E.W. (Spring 1991). "Rethinking Literacy." *Educational Horizons* 69, 3: 120–128.

Gardner, H. (1983). *Frames of Mind: The Theory of Multiple Intelligences*. New York: Harper and Row.

Fuller, T., ed. (1989). *The Voice of Liberal Learning: Michael Oakeshott on Education*. New Haven, Conn.: Yale University Press.

Harris, I.B. (1993). "New Expectations for Professional Skills: Reflective Practice and Self-Correction." In *Education for the Professions*, edited by L. Cunny and J. Wemjin. San Francisco: Jossey-Bass.

Joyce, B., and M. Weil, with B. Showers (1992). *Models of Teaching*. 4th ed. Needham Heights, Mass.: Allyn and Bacon.

Kolb, D.A. (1984). *Experiential Learning*. Englewood Cliffs, N.J.: Prentice-Hall.

Mezirow, J., and Associates (1990). *Fostering Critical Reflection in Adulthood*. San Francisco: Jossey-Bass.

Pratt, F. (n.d.). *Teaching About Aging*. ERIC Clearinghouse for Social Studies/Social Science Education and Social Science Education Consortium, Inc., Boulder, Colo. (ED 135682).

Resnick, L.B., and L.E. Klopfer. (1989). "Toward the Thinking Curriculum: an Overview." In *Toward the Thinking Curriculum*, edited by L.B. Resnick and L.E. Klopfer. Alexandria, Va.: ASCD.

Schon, D.A. (1983). *The Reflective Practitioner: How Professionals Think in Action*. New York: Basic Books, Inc.

Schon, D.A. (1987). *Educating the Reflective Practitioner: Toward a New Design for Teaching and Learning in the Professions*. San Francisco: Jossey-Bass.

Silcox, H. (1993). *A How-to Guide to Reflection: Adding Cognitive Learning to Community Service Programs*. Philadelphia: Brighton Press.

Tulving, E. (1983). *Elements of Episodic Memory*. Oxford: Oxford University Press.

Conclusion:
Challenges for the Future

Kate McPherson, Director, Project Service Leadership,
Vancouver, Washington

Carol W. Kinsley, Director, Community Service Learning Center,
Springfield, Massachusetts

Service learning is both a mindset and a pedagogy. As a mindset, it views young people as resources who have the capacity and energies to contribute to their schools and communities. As a mindset, it influences how we design instruction and programs. It helps democratize our schools and communities by giving voice and influence to young people who are often the recipients of service, but are rarely asked to be "of" service.

As a pedagogy, service learning is an effective way of teaching citizenship and community problem-solving skills. By giving students authentic learning experiences, service learning also provides a powerful way of connecting any content area to the community through study and action.

The exemplary practices described here demonstrate how people have begun to tap these potentials. We hope these stories illustrate not so much *how* one implements, but rather *why* service learning is important and how a vision for service learning can transform classroom teaching and provide a meaningful vehicle for school reform. In some instances, the stories demonstrate that as service learning becomes part of the culture of a school, it becomes such a natural part of the educational process that it is not always labeled, but is recognized as a meaningful way to teach and learn.

At the same time, practitioners who implement service learning often find new challenges as they work with students to determine the direction of the service experiences and the preparation needed to make these experiences successful. The significance of these challenges underscores the importance of this "mindset pedagogy" and the considerations that need to be addressed when implementing curriculum and programs. For instance:

• Those who seek to "serve" may be asked to work with people different from themselves. Without sufficient understanding, their service experiences may simply reinforce old stereotypes and perpetuate a duality between server and recipient, between the helpless and the helpful. Such a posture can perpetuate a sense of paternalism. As educators develop service learning, they need to establish ways to build sensitivity and understanding toward relationships that cross traditional ethnic and socioeconomic barriers.

• We cannot use the community for service learning without actually addressing significant issues. Programs need to enable youth to examine real problems in meaningful ways and to grapple with policy and social justice issues. Through service-learning activities, students can explore ways to prevent problems rather than perpetuate the need for direct service.

• Service learning runs the danger of becoming simply another activity that is trivialized through repetition and raped of its emotion as we make it safe for children. As schools move to institutionalize service learning to provide continuity and support, we recognize the importance of the generative energy of invention and serendipity and the creative possibilities they inspire.

• Educators need to clarify the deeper motivations that guide their interest in service learning. Without such clarity, programs will not have the integrity they need.

• As schools work with communities to develop service-learning programs, the challenge is to develop a community that educates and effectively shares its talents and information with students. Communities as well as schools must become facilitators of learning. Schools must work collaboratively with parents and with civic, ethnic, religious, social service, and other organizations to share responsibility for the education of our young people.

These challenges are not meant to disarm but to reenergize our educating institutions. As we engage in these challenges, we learn and grow as individuals. Education gains a broader context; and the African proverb, "It takes a village to raise a child," gains meaning and life.

Part VI

Resources

Service-Learning Resources

Community Service Learning Centers

Community Service Learning Center
333 Bridge St.
Springfield, MA 01103
Telephone: (413) 734-6857. Fax: (413) 747-5368

Mather Career Center
University of Massachusetts at Amherst
Amherst, MA 01003
Telephone: (413) 545-6380. Fax: (413) 545-4426

Project Service Leadership
12703 N.W. 20th Ave.
Vancouver, WA 98685
Telephone: (206) 576-5070. Fax: (206) 576-5068

National Organizations

The following organizations offer national training and opportunities to network with other service-learning teachers. Additional organizations are noted as founding members of the Alliance for Service Learning in Educational Reform in this section.

National Service-Learning Cooperative: ServeAmerica K–12 Clearinghouse

A national database of programs, trainers, peer consultants, and resources has been developed for educators, community organizations and students. The National Cooperative includes eight Regional Technical Assistance Centers, located strategically across the country, which provide assistance regionally. The Clearinghouse is located at the University of Minnesota Vocational and Technical Education Building, 1954 Buford Avenue, R-290, St. Paul, MN 55108. Telephone: 1-800-808-SERVE. Internet E-mail: serve@maroon.tc.umn.edu

National Youth Leadership Council (NYLC)

Local, regional, and national staff development is offered to educators, youth professionals, and all those interested in youth service. NYLC, 1910 West County Rd. B, St. Paul, MN 55113-1337. Telephone: (612) 631-3672.

National Society for Experiential Education (NSEE)
NSEE is a community of individuals, institutions, and organizations which believe in and practice experiential education. Membership offers a quarterly newsletter, special interest forums; discounts for their national conference, national consultants, a national resource center referral for experiential education and service learning, and publications. NSEE, 3509 Haworth Drive, Suite 207, Raleigh, NC 227609-72299. Telephone: (919) 767-3263.

National Center for Service Learning in Early Adolescence (NCSLEA)
The Center offers technical assistance, training and program development, and a variety of resource materials for middle-grade educators and policymakers. NCSLEA, CASE/CUNY, 25 W. 43rd St., Suite 612, New York, NY 10036-8099. Telephone: (212) 642-2946.

Resource Books and Other Materials

The following by no means represent an exhaustive list of service-learning resources. For additional resources, contact the ServeAmerica K–12 Clearinghouse at 1-800-808-SERVE. Internet E-mail: serve@maroon.tc.umn.edu.

General Service Learning Resources
• *Design, Leadership, and Models: The Change Agents of School Service-Learning Programs* (1994). Harry Silcox's latest book provides model program descriptions and strategies to use in the development of service-learning programs. Brighton Press, Inc., 64 Lempa Rd., Holland, PA 18966.
• *Growing Hope: A Sourcebook on Integrating Service into the School Curriculum,* edited by Rich Willits Cairn and Jim Kielsmeier (1991). Offers background, definitions, rationale, nuts-and-bolts implementation, sample program materials, and resource materials. National Youth Leadership Council, 1910 West County Rd. B, Roseville, MN 55113. Telephone: (612) 631-3672.
•*Service-Learning: Getting to the Heart of School Renewal, A Guide for Implementing School-Based Service-Learning* (1994). School Improvement Project, 12730 N.W. 20th Ave., Vancouver, WA 98685. Telephone: (360) 576-5070. $7.

Grades K–8
• *Adventures of Adolescents,* by Catherine A. Rolzinski (1990). Explores the experiences of seven middle school youth service programs. Checks payable to Youth Service America, 1319 F St., N.W., Suite 900, Washington, DC 20004. $14.
• *Kid's Guide to Social Action,* by Barbara A. Lewis (1991). Classroom guide to solving social problems and turning creative thinking into positive action. Free Spirit Publishing, 400 First Avenue N, Suite 616, Minneapolis, MN 55401-1724. Telephone: 1-800-735-7323. $14.95 + $3.25 S&H.
• *Learning by Giving.* Curriculum for K–8 Service (April 1993). Filled with lesson plans and resource materials on how to integrate service into curriculum. National Youth Leadership Council, 1910 West County Rd. B, Roseville, MN 55113. $45.

• *Routes to Reform: Service-Learning K–8 Curriculum Ideas* (1994). Written by teachers from Generator Schools, a National Service Learning Initiative Project sponsored by the National Youth Leadership Council. 1910 West County Rd. B, Roseville, MN 55113. Telephone: (612) 631-3672. $15.

• *Skills for Adolescence (6–8)* (1992). Quest International. Lions-Quest curriculum specifically helps teachers reinforce and enrich critical assets of young people's lives through comprehensive classroom curriculum focusing on life skills, active citizenship, and service to others. To use it you must attend a three-day workshop near your city. Cost is approximately $400 for each person; cost includes training, curriculum, and meals. To order, call Quest International, 537 Jones Rd., P.O. Box 566, Granville, OH 43023-0566. Telephone: 1- 800-446-2700. Fax: (614) 522-6580.

• *Standing Tall Teaching Guide*, Grades 6–8 (1992). Activities that can be used by a classroom or club that teaches the steps of powerful social action. It includes stories of "giraffes," people who stick their necks out to help the community. The Giraffe Project, P.O. Box 759, Langley, WA 98620. Telephone: (206) 321-0757. $95.

• *Things That Work in Community Service Learning* (1995). A series of monographs describing successful middle school experiences in every content area. They are written by teachers based on real curriculum units. For list and prices, contact the Community Service Learning Center, 333 Bridge St., Springfield, MA 01103. Telephone: (413) 734-6857. Fax: (413) 747-5368.

• *VYTAL* (Volunteer Youth Training and Leadership) (1993). A comprehensive collection of activities that enable students to see the value of service and to develop specific action plans. Manual available from VYTAL, c/o Greater Pittsburgh Camp Fire Council, 730 River Ave., Suite 531, Pittsburgh, PA 15212. Telephone: (412) 231-6004. $30.

• *Whole Learning Through Service: A Guide for Integrating Service, K–8* (1990). The curriculum provides teachers with community service learning experiences that can be used to generate learning in content areas. Order guide from The Community Service Learning Center, 333 Bridge St., Springfield, MA 01103. Telephone: (413) 734-6857. Fax: (413) 747-5368. $25 (Check payable to Springfield Public Schools).

High School

• *150 Ways Teens Can Make a Difference*, by Mariam Salzman and Teresa Reisgies (1991). The information contains steps for taking action and a comprehensive list of action plans and organizations. Peterson's Guides, Princeton, New Jersey. Telephone: (800) 388-3282.

• *ACT—Active Citizenship Today* (1995). Active Citizenship Today (ACT) is a new service-learning project for middle and high school students, jointly planned and implemented by the Close-Up Foundation and the Constitutional Rights Foundation. The four-year project will integrate community service and the study of public policy into the social studies curriculum. Call Close-up at (703) 706-3640 or the Constitutional Rights Foundation at (213) 487-5590. Cost: Student edition: $12.95. Teacher's Guide: $17.95 + S&H.

• *Coordinator's Handbook* (1989). Provides a step-by-step process to help school staff develop a community service program. Lincoln Filene Center's Community Service Learning Program (CSLP), Tufts University, Medford, MA 02155. Telephone: (617) 641-3858. Fax: (617) 627-3401. $20.

• *Enriching Learning Through Service* (1989). Provides a summary of the research that supports service and provides specific examples of how teachers have enriched their classroom learning through service. Project Service Leadership, 12703 N.W. 20th Avenue, Vancouver, WA 98685. Telephone: (206) 576-5070. Fax: (206) 576-7068. $12.50 + $2.50 (S&H) payable to the "School Improvement Project."

• *High School Curriculum* (May 1993). A course curriculum that includes units on aging, disabilities, homelessness, and environment. Maryland Student Service Alliance, Maryland State Department of Education, 200 West Baltimore St., Baltimore, MD 21201. Telephone: (410) 767-0358. $20.

• *Quest: Skills for Action* (1994). The material provides a student magazine for $2.95. For 30 to 500 students, $2.80. Required training is $435. To order, call Quest International, 537 Jones Rd., P.O. Box 566, Granville, OH 43023-0566. Telephone: 1(800) 446-2700. Fax: (614) 522-6580.

Reflection

• *A How-to Guide to Reflection*. This book, written by Harry Silcox (1993), explores the service-learning movement and the use of reflective teaching as a critical component to blend experience with school curriculums. Brighton Press Inc., 64 Lempa Rd., Holland, PA 18966. $12.

• *Learning Through Service* (1989). This guide helps teachers and community advisors more effectively facilitate discussions and reflective activities. Project Service Leadership, 12703 N.W. 20th Avenue, Vancouver, WA 98685. Telephone: (206) 576-5070. Fax: (206) 576-7068. $5.50 + $2.50 (S&H) payable to the "School Improvement Project."

• *Reflection: The Key to Service Learning* (1991). This book outlines the ways reflection may be used to transform a community service project into a quality learning experience. It includes rationale, sample activities and steps for integrating reflection into a service learning program. National Center for Service Learning in Early Adolescence, CASE/CUNY, 25 W. 43rd St., Suite 612, New York, NY 10036-8099. Telephone: (212) 642-2946. $15.

Special Populations

• *Special Education Curriculum* (December 1993). Maryland Student Service Alliance, Maryland State Department of Education, 200 West Baltimore St., Baltimore, MD 21201. Telephone: (410) 767-0358. $20 (payable to Maryland Student Service Alliance).

• *Something Shining Like Gold . . . But Better* (1991). A manual for the National Indian Youth Leadership Program's nationally successfu, intensive leadership program for Indian youth. National Youth Leadership Council, 1910 West County Rd. B, Roseville, MN 55113. Telephone: (612) 631-3672.

Peer Assistance

- *Becoming a Friendly Helper: A Handbook for Student Facilitators*, by Robert D. Myrick and Robert P. Bowman (1981). Educational Media Corporation, P.O. Box 21311, Minneapolis, MN 55421.

- *Partner's Program: A Guide for Teachers and Program Leaders* (1991). Includes specific planning and training steps that are necessary for effective intergenerational programs for middle school youth. National Center for Service Learning in Early Adolescence, CASE/CUNY, 25 W. 43rd St., Suite 612, New York, NY 10036-8099. Telephone: (212) 642-2946. $20.

Liability

- *No Surprises: Controlling Risks in Volunteer Programs*, by Charles Tremper and Gwynee Kostin (1993). Nonprofit Risk Management Center, 1001 Connecticut Avenue, N.W., Suite 900, Washington, DC 20036. $12.95 includes postage.

Videos

- *Citizen Stories* (1991). Focuses on five individuals of varying ages and backgrounds who opted for action over apathy. The accompanying guide includes activities to lead students to ponder the meaning and varied aspects of social responsibility. Closeup Foundation, 44 Canal Plaza, Alexandria, VA 22314. Telephone: 1-800-765-3131. $60 + (S&H).

- *The Courage to Care: The Strength to Serve . . .* (1994). Maryland Student Service Alliance, Maryland State Department of Education, 200 West Baltimore St., Baltimore, MD 21201. Telephone: (410) 767-0358. $12.50 (payable to Maryland Student Service Alliance).

- *Hearts and Minds Engaged* (1994). Shows examples of middle and high school service-learning programs in Washington State. West Publishing Company, School Division D4-13, 620 Opperman Dr., P.O. Box 64779, St. Paul, MN 55164-0779. Telephone: (612) 687-7482. $39.95. Accompanying text: *Community Service Learning Guide*, $16.95. Costs subject to change.

- *Routes to Reform: Service-Learning K–8 Curriculum Ideas* (1994). This video takes a close look at three exemplary programs in elementary, middle, and senior high schools across the United States. National Youth Leadership Council, 1910 West County Rd. B, Roseville, MN 55113. Telephone: (612) 631-3672. $15.

The *Service Learning Planning and Resource Guide*: A Description

Barbara Gomez, Council of Chief State School Officers,
Washington, D.C.

The Council of Chief State School Officers' (CCSSO) 1993 publication, the *Service Learning Planning and Resource Guide*, is intended to encourage states, schools, and communities to examine the common goals and outcomes of hundreds of education, training, and youth development programs and to craft and work toward a comprehensive vision for those programs through service learning. The publication is based on the premise that all education and youth development programs should be centered around one common vision of what we want all young people to know and be able to do, including the desired knowledge, skills, competencies, attitudes, values, and behavior to prepare them for informed citizenship, healthy lifestyles, and productive employment.

As articulated by CCSSO in its 1992 policy statement, "Student Success Through Collaboration," we must redefine the notion of student success to include not only intellectual competencies but also the physical, emotional, and social well-being of children and youth. The publication attempts to show, through actual examples, the power of service learning and its potential to foster the intellectual, social, and emotional well-being of children and youth in a holistic way.

The first section of the *Service Learning Planning and Resource Guide* profiles more than 100 federal programs that can be tapped to develop and expand school-based, districtwide, and state-level service-learning-related activities. The profiles identify legislative sources, eligibility criteria, level of appropriations, allowable uses of funds, and experiential learning initiatives in 40 states. The guide targets 15 federal agencies for service-learning initiatives related to school improvement, arts and humanities, health and human services, math and science, school-to-work programs, literacy, environment, and violence prevention. The second section of the guide identifies the service-learning-related resources and services of more than 25 national and regional organizations.

The *Service Learning Planning and Resource Guide* is unique because it is a "living document." It is "living" because its content represents the continuing process of collaboration. It describes how education systems are working with local, state, and federal agencies, foundations, businesses, community-based organizations, labor unions, youth-serving organizations, professional associations, and private nonprofits to improve education via service learning. Second, it is "living" because its contents will constantly change—legislation will undergo reauthorization, federal programs will lose their appropriations, new programs and organizations will be created, and new resources will emerge. Third, it is "living" because it represents the efforts of real leaders—teachers, students, and a variety of other educators and professionals—who have a powerful vision to involve young people as resources in their schools and communities while developing and enhancing their intellectual, social, emotional, and physical well-being. Finally, it is "living" because service learning is a dynamic process. Through service learning, communities and schools work together to address needs, discover new issues, ask new questions, and design new solutions.

The *Service Learning Planning and Resource Guide* is $15.00 and can be obtained from CCSSO, One Massachusetts Avenue, N.W., Suite 700, Washington, DC 20001-1431. Telephone: (202) 336-7016.

Standards of Quality for School-Based Service Learning

Alliance for Service Learning in Education Reform (May 1993)

What Is Service Learning?

Service learning is a method by which young people learn and develop through active participation in thoughtfully organized service experiences . . .

- That meet actual community needs.
- That are coordinated in collaboration with the school and community.
- That are integrated into each young person's academic curriculum.
- That provide structured time for a young person to think, talk, and write about what he/she did and saw during the actual service activity.
- That provide young people with opportunities to use newly acquired academic skills and knowledge in real life situations in their own communities.
- That enhance what is taught in the school by extending student learning beyond the classroom.
- That help to foster the development of a sense of caring for others.

The Standards

I. Effective service-learning efforts strengthen service and academic learning.

II. Model service learning provides concrete opportunities for youth to learn new skills, to think critically, and to test new roles in an environment which encourages risk-taking and rewards competence.

III. Preparation and reflection are essential elements in service learning.

IV. Students' efforts are recognized by their peers and the community they serve.

V. Youth are involved in the planning.

VI. The service students perform makes a meaningful contribution to the community.

VII. Effective service learning integrates systematic formative and summative evaluation.

VIII. Service learning connects school and its community in new and positive ways.

IX. Service learning is understood and supported as an integral element in the life of a school and its community.

X. Skilled adult guidance and supervision is essential to the success of service learning.

XI. Preservice and staff development which includes the philosophy and methodology of service learning best ensure that program quality and continuity are maintained.

Introduction

Community service is a powerful tool for youth development. It transforms the young person from a passive recipient to an active provider, and in so doing redefines the perception of youth in the community from a cause of problems to a source of solutions. When combined with formal education, service becomes a method of learning or "service learning."

Service learning enables teachers to employ a variety of effective teaching strategies that emphasize student-centered, interactive, experiential education. Service learning places curricular concepts in the context of real-life situations and empowers students to analyze, evaluate, and synthesize these concepts through practical problem-solving, often in service to the community.

In setting forth standards of quality for school-based service learning, we do not presume to provide a list of absolutes, nor even a complete inventory of the elements that contribute to high quality. Instead, what follows is designed to serve as a yardstick that can be used to measure the success of a variety of approaches to service learning, locally as well as nationally.

We are aware of the wide diversity among our schools, their students, and their communities, and have tried to enunciate criteria broad enough to be applied across varied regions and populations, yet concrete enough to be translated into action.

Service learning connects young people to the community, placing them in challenging situations where they associate with adults and accumulate experiences that can strengthen traditional academic studies. Service learning also makes classroom study relevant, as young people connect their actions in the world beyond the school's walls with work in math, social studies, language arts, and science.

Young people have few opportunities to be around adults outside of school and home. As described in "A Matter of Time," a report of the Task Force on Youth Development and Community Programs of the Carnegie Corporation (1992), too many children are raising each other with little stabilizing input from adults.

The isolation of young people has resulted in a rift between them and society's institutions. Service learning involves youth in active roles in the community, and establishes a new relationship between young people and an adult facilitator; hence it can be a powerful force in closing that rift.

As they work together for a defined purpose, youth and adults will learn to respect each other. When mutual trust is established between adults and young people, meaningful dialogue, so often absent in the life of today's youth, can take place.

Although the terms are sometimes used interchangeably, service learning and community service are not synonymous. Community service may be, and often is, a powerful experience for young people, but community service becomes service learning when there is a deliberate connection made between service and learning opportunities which are then accompanied by conscious and thoughtfully designed occasions for reflecting on the service experience.

127

Reflection may be described as the process of looking back on the implications of actions taken—both good and bad—determining what has been gained, lost, or achieved, and connecting these conclusions to future actions and larger societal contexts.

Effective service learning responds to the needs of the community as well as to the developmental and learning needs of youth. The model should be modified to reflect the maturity and capacities of youth at different stages. Duration of the service role, type of service, desired outcomes, and the structure for reflection must all be designed to be age-appropriate. Service learning is most effective when it combines community needs and students' interests, and is compatible with their skills and abilities.

I. Effective service learning efforts strengthen service and academic learning.

Service-learning efforts should begin with clearly articulated learning goals, to be achieved through structured preparation and reflection—discussion, writing, reading, observation—and the service itself. Learning goals—knowledge, skills, attitudes—must be compatible with the developmental level of the young person.

The examples that follow demonstrate that service can be linked to academics in many ways, and at all levels. Even in the primary grades, when the youngest children are learning about their own neighborhood, they can engage in conservation or recycling projects. Children in elementary school might plan safe routes for the walk to and from school to develop mathematics, observation and map skills. In secondary school, adolescents can explore issues such as hunger through virtually every academic discipline: crop rotation and rainfall in science and geography, computing individual and collective nutritional needs in math class, the economies of food distribution and efforts of governments to address these problems in social studies, and so on. Service at a food distribution center could reinforce all this learning by placing it in the context of community needs.

II. Model service learning provides concrete opportunities for youth to learn new skills, to think critically, and to test new roles in an environment which encourages risk-taking and rewards competence.

The experience of service in the community, however laudable, is not an end in itself. By performing meaningful work, young people can develop and apply new skills, try on different roles, and plan—constantly reinforcing connections between classroom learning and the real world.

In making the world their laboratory, service learning has the potential to enable students to develop increased self-reliance in real settings. They learn to work cooperatively, and to relate to peers and adults in new and constructive ways. Their self-image improves in a legitimate way, not because of imagined good feelings but rather as a result of increased competence.

Students who work at a senior center learn about aging, the demographics of a community, its available social services, government policy, history, and human relations. Those who help supervise young children at a day care center learn about child development, parenting, and social policy. School students who develop a plan for school recycling and investigate local services develop an understanding of the promise of recycling as well as the problems it poses.

III. Preparation and reflection are essential elements in service learning.

The essential elements that give service learning its educational integrity are preparation and reflection. Preparatory study of underlying problems, history, and policies enriches student learning, as do deliberate discussion and other classroom activities. Preparation also should introduce the skills and attitudes needed for the service to be effective.

Reflection is the framework in which students process and synthesize the information and ideas they have gained through their service experience and in the classroom. Through the process of reflection, students analyze concepts, evaluate experiences and form opinions, all in the context of the school curricula.

IV. Students' efforts will be recognized by their peers and the community they serve.

In large and small ways during the period of service as well as with a culminating event, students will share with the community and their peers what has been gained and gained and given through service. Recognizing the work that children and youth perform reinforces the significance of the enterprise and the worth of the young people.

V. Youth are involved in the planning.

When young people are given the opportunity to work in after-school and senior centers, tutoring young children, or leading an effort to clean up a local stream, they are being entrusted with important work with the expectation that they have the ability to perform it. Building that trust is essential to the success of the effort. That is why it is critical to involve young people at the very beginning of the work. Moreover it provides teachers with important opportunities to encourage curiosity and to foster planning and analytical skills.

Just as it is necessary to build consensus and support for any group effort in the adult world, it is also necessary to gain the support of young people in reaching out to the community.

VI. The service students perform contributes in a meaningful way to the community. *(In this context, the school may be defined as the community.)*

The service roles or projects that involve students in service learning will differ widely, depending upon the age of the young people, the needs of the community, and the specific learning goals that have been determined. However, whatever the activity, the following features are shared by high quality approaches:

• The work must be *real*; it must fill a recognized need, whether in the school or in the outside community.

• The service activity must be developmentally appropriate. Fox example, a districtwide K–12 effort to refurbish a park could consist of the following projects: Younger primary students study plants, grow flowers from seeds, and plant them in the park. Older primary students research what types of birds live in the park's trees, and build bird houses or feeding stations which they continue to maintain throughout the year.

Intermediate-age students extend the school's recycling program to the park—learning about and working with city agencies to institute it, decorating collection bins, and designing posters to increase community awareness. In health sciences, high school students design and build an exercise path; in art class they create a mural for park buildings; in social studies they survey the community to find out what members would like the park to be used for and report their findings to the appropriate government agency. A tangible or visible outcome or product results from the service and when possible demonstrate, the learning outcomes.

VII. Effective service learning integrates systematic formative and summative evaluation.

All learning programs, especially relatively new ones, can benefit from systematic evaluation. While anecdotal evidence of a program's effectiveness is useful, more systematic methods for assessing the impacts of service learning are needed, particularly since the field of service learning is growing rapidly and demand for in-depth understanding of program models and approaches is high.

Such assessment includes detailed documentation of program components and processes; the outcomes identified by, and expected of, all participants (i.e. students, community members, schools); and the impact of the service-learning program on individual participants, schools, and community.

Assessment processes can vary in extent and complexity, depending on the nature of the questions asked and on available time and resources. For example, if one question is, "Do students' attitudes toward school change as a result of involvement in service learning?" attitudinal measures can be taken at various points, or indirect measures such as school attendance can be used.

A question like "How does service learning affect civic responsibility?" would require measures which assess components of civic responsibility such as values, behaviors, and attitudes to be administered over an extended period of time. If the question is "In what ways can the experiential learning pedagogies associated with service learning help to bring about education reform?" then assessment methods need to focus on the relationship between experiential teaching techniques and their multiple effects on learning and development.

A major benefit of formative (on-going) assessment is program improvement. Ongoing data supplies necessary information regarding program design in relation to program purpose and pinpoints where modification might be necessary or desirable.

Summative assessment also affects program development, and in addition provides aggregate information on the overall effectiveness of a particular program model. A combination of formative and summative assessment, whether done on a small or large scale, helps to ensure that programs remain responsive to their purposes and participants.

VIII. Service learning connects school and its community in new and positive ways.

Service-learning has the potential to reduce the barriers that often separate school and community. Students learn that they can move beyond their small circle of peers and take their place as contributing members of the community as they discover that learning occurs throughout the community in traditional and non-traditional settings—libraries, public agencies, parks, hospitals, etc. Relations are enhanced as agencies, citizens, and local government officials find that their expertise and counsel is sought by the school. Through service learning, schools and communities become genuine partners in the education and development of youth.

Just as school administrators have an obligation to support the coordinated implementation of service learning in the community, the community must be committed to supporting service learning in the schools. Communities must recognize and respect the curricular goals strengthened in the schools by service learning. Communities must work with the schools to ensure that students' service opportunities are structured to be consistent with learner outcomes.

IX. Service learning is understood and supported as an integral element in the life of a school and its community.

In order for service learning to be accepted and succeeded in any setting, it must receive institutional support for its philosophy and its financial requirements. School-based service learning needs the support of both district and building administrators. Too often, educators enthusiastic about service learning are offered token support, largely in words of praise for the "wonderful work" that is accomplished.

While spoken recognition is important, what is significant is the provision of the time that goes into exemplary service learning. Teachers who implement service learning, either as a discrete class, as a part of their subject area lessons, or with thematic or inter-disciplinary learning, must be supported with planning and implementation time as well as a reasonable budget for student incentives, expenses such as transportation, and other outside resources that can be crucial to the success of the effort.

Outside the classroom, the development, implementation, and coordination of service projects in the community require a level of support that must extend beyond the efforts of any individual or group of teachers. Service learning can enhance school-community partnerships, but to do so, it must be presented to the community in a manner that does not conflict with community interests.

To ensure the stability of these school-community partnerships, schools/districts implementing service learning must provide continuing and visible oversight as well as coordination among community interests and classroom teachers.

Administrators should ensure that the climate of the school is open to service learning. Even those who are not directly involved in service learning should understand its significance.

Teachers and students must understand why some students have different schedules and may appear to be receiving special treatment as a result of doing service. The whole school community must be aware of the learning and service goals which enable students to pursue these goals.

Similarly, when there are placement sites, even those who do not have direct contact with students must understand and welcome the young people. Students' roles must be clearly articulated and their tasks carefully defined with the awareness of the administration and clients of the agency so that the work the youth perform is respected.

The learning and service goals must be clearly defined and understood by all involved.

Parents play a critical role in the service-learning equation. At the minimum, their permission must be obtained in order for the young people to serve.

But they must be brought into the process at an early enough stage so that they fully support the notion of service and the unique learning opportunities that service provides.

Communication of the benefits of service and its impact on attitude toward school, and the relationship between work and service, should be communicated so that support from the home is forthcoming. Service also provides a wide variety of options for parental involvement, as students learn about the community of which their parents are adult members.

Parents with busy schedules might offer ideas of resources or potential placement sites, and when appropriate share with the students how their work and volunteer experience affect the larger community.

X. Skilled adult guidance and supervision are essential to the success of service learning.

The case for service learning is compelling, but the task is a complicated one to sustain. Teachers employing service learning in their classrooms should have opportunities for professional development. They must be given the tools, the training, and the technical assistance necessary to implement meaningful service-learning experiences.

Issues of type of service, site selection, curriculum connections, reflection, recognition, tangible outcomes, and evaluation must be considered along with the ever-present concerns of insurance, liability, and logistics.

Learning takes place during the preparation and while serving and reflecting. Youth must be afforded supportive supervision at placement sites. Supervision at the site should extend beyond the basic elements of taking attendance and keeping track of hours worked.

With such rich opportunities for youth to grow, to learn about others, and to take on responsibility, a caring person must assume responsibility for overseeing youth activities and support these efforts.

XI. Pre-service training and staff development which include the philosophy and methodology of service learning best ensure that program quality and continuity are maintained.

If service learning is to assume real importance in educating students for the 21st century, it must be incorporated into pre-service and in-service training and staff development. It will be critically important, especially in this transitional period as service learning begins to find a place in the educational process, to provide high quality training.

Many of the teaching strategies and behaviors essential to high quality in school-based service learning are in sharp contrast to what has been taught in "methods" courses. It will not be enough to offer course work at educational institutions; potential teachers should engage in service learning as part of their own training.

Founding Members of the Alliance for Service Learning in Educational Reform

These standards of quality for school-based service learning were compiled for the Alliance for Service Learning in Education Reform by the Standards Committee. In the following list, Standards Committee members are identified by an asterisk. Final editing of the Standards was courtesy of SerVermont.

American Youth Foundation
  Bob MacArthur
American Youth Policy Forum
  Sam Halperin
Association of Junior Leagues
  Kathy Herre (*)
California Department of Education
  Wade Brynelson
  Bernadette Chi
Campus Compact
  Keith Morton
City Volunteer Corps of New York
  Toni Schmiegelow
Clark/Atlanta University
  Bill Denton
Close Up Foundation
  Frank Dirks
Colorado Department of Education
  Elaine Andrus
  Richard Laughlin
Community Service Learning Center
  Carol Kinsley
Constitutional Rights Foundation
  Todd Clark
  Kathleen Kirby
  Ingrid Sausjord

Council of Chief State School
  Officers
  Barbara Gomez (*)
Eagle Rock School
  Robert Burkhardt
East Bay Conservation Corps
  Joanna Lennon
Groveport Madison LINK
  Lana Borders
Maryland Student Service Alliance
  Maggie O'Neill
  Kathleen Kennedy Townsend (*)
National Center for Service
  Learning
  in Early Adolescence
  Alice Halsted (*Chair)
  Joan Schine (*)
National Center for Service
  Learning and School Change
  Louise Guigliano
National Society for Experiential
  Education
  Alan Wurtzdorff(*)
National Youth Leadership Council
  Rich Cairn (*)
  Jim Kielsmeier

New Jersey Department of Higher Education
Martin Friedman

PennSERVE
John Briscoe

Pennsylvania Department of Education
Jean diSabatino

Pennsylvania Institute for Environmental and Community Service Learning
Harry Silcox (*)

Points of Light Foundation
Chuck Supple

Project Service Leadership
Kate McPherson

Quest International
Mike Buscemi

SerVermont
Cynthia Parsons

Thomas Jefferson Forum, Tufts University
Patricia Barnicle
Mark Saunders

University of Minnesota
Rob Shumer

University of Pittsburgh
Joanne Long

Vermont Department of Education
Sheila Bailey

West Virginia Department of Education
Jack Newhouse

Youth Engaged in Service
Nancy Powell

Youth Service America
Frank Slobig

Youth Volunteer Corps of America
David Battey

Unaffiliated Member
Cathryn Berger Kaye (*)

Seasons of Service

Corporation for National and Community Service

I challenge a new generation of young Americans to a season of service. . . . There is so much to be done—enough, indeed, for millions of others who are still young in spirit to give of themselves in service, too.
—President Bill Clinton, Inaugural Address

The President's national service legislation created the new Corporation for National and Community Service. Formed in conjunction with the White House Office of National Service, built upon the foundation of the former Commission on National and Community Service and incorporating the new Civilian Community Corps, the Corporation is positioned to revitalize service in every region and community across the country.

The Corporation supports a range of national and community service programs, providing opportunities for participants to serve full-time and part-time, as volunteers or as stipended participants, and as individuals or as a part of a team. From our youngest citizens engaged in service-learning activities in grades K–12, to our older Americans assisting those in need in their communities, the Corporation provides "seasons of service" for all Americans.

Americorps

Americorps is the President's national service vision of directly and demonstrably addressing the nation's education, human, public safety, and environmental needs at the community level. AmeriCorps offers opportunities for Americans age 17 or older to make a substantial commitment to serve their country and to earn education awards for college or vocational training in return. Up to 20,000 Americans of all backgrounds will serve full-time or part-time in the program's first year, beginning in the fall of 1994.

• Included in AmeriCorps will be the more than 1,000 young people serving in the new *Civilian Community Corps*. The CCC is a national residential service option in which participants are housed and trained together on military bases and deployed as teams to community service sites. The CCC combines the best of our military tradition with the best practices of local community service corps, providing participants with opportunities to solve real community needs while developing their own leadership skills and receiving invaluable training for future careers.

• *Volunteers in Service to America (VISTA)* will also be an important component of AmeriCorps. VISTA is a full-time, year-long program for men and women age 18 and older who commit themselves to increasing the capability of low-income people to improve the conditions of their own lives. VISTA volunteers serve in rural or urban areas or on Indian reservations, sharing their skills and experience in fields such as employment training, literacy, shelter for the homeless, and neighborhood revitalization. Approximately 3,500 VISTA volunteers are currently serving, joining more than 100,000 alumni who have previously served their country through VISTA.

Learn and Serve America

Learn and Serve America programs are school-based, and integrate service into daily academic life. Service learning is a method by which young people learn and develop through active participation in service experiences that meet community needs, and foster a lifetime commitment to service.

• *School and Community-Based Programs* support schools and nonprofit organizations that engage school-aged youth in active learning through service. By the fall of 1994, over 300,000 youth in all 50 states will participate in programs which will provide opportunities for them to analyze classroom learning and community issues, and apply their new knowledge and skills to meaningful service activities. As a central element of the learning experiences of young people, service learning will enhance academic achievement and foster personal growth while empowering youth to make a difference in communities across the country.

• *Higher Education Innovation Programs* engage college students in meeting pressing community needs. Higher education projects support high-quality community service and service-learning initiatives at colleges and universities across the nation. Some are student-run; some are faculty-led; many are integrated with academic study. As essential parts of the college experience, these efforts will create a new generation of leaders committed to service.

National Senior Service Corps

The National Senior Service Corps utilizes the skills, talents, and experience of older Americans in addressing urgent issues facing the nation. Together, the following programs involve 470,000 volunteers who serve in 1,223 local projects and devote an annual total of over 111 million hours of service to their local communities.

• The *Foster Grandparent Program* offers low-income persons age 60 and over the opportunity to serve one-on-one with children and young people who have special needs, including teen parents, boarder babies and those who are abused and neglected. Over 23,000 Foster Grandparents serve twenty hours a week in volunteer stations such as hospitals, public schools, day care centers, and correctional institutions.

• The *Senior Companion Program* volunteers are low-income men and women age 60 and over. Senior Companions provide individualized support and assistance to other adults, primarily the homebound elderly. Their services help the homebound achieve and maintain their highest level of independent living.

Approximately 13,000 Senior Companions provide disability assistance, home management assistance, and social and recreational companionship to approximately 32,000 individuals each year.

• The *Retired and Senior Volunteer Program (RSVP)* is a network of 430,000 Americans, age 55 and up, who perform a wide range of volunteer services that meet real community needs and effectively use their skills, interests, and experience. RSVP is the Corporation's largest service program, providing communities with volunteers diverse in experience, interest, income, and education, and ready to take on the challenges facing the country.

For information contact:

Corporation for National Service
1201 New York Ave., N.W.
Washington, DC 20525
Telephone: (202) 606-5000, ext. 115
Fax: (202) 606-4906

About the Authors

Editors of This Book

Carol W. Kinsley, *Director, Community Service Learning Center, Springfield, Massachusetts.* Address: Community Service Learning Center, 333 Bridge St., Springfield, MA 01103. Telephone: (413) 734-6857. Fax: (413) 747-5368.

Kate McPherson, *Director, Project Service Leadership, Vancouver, Washington.* Address: 12703 N.W. 20th Ave., Vancouver, WA 98685. Telephone: (206) 576-5070. Fax: (206) 576-5068

Kinsley and McPherson provide technical assistance, teacher training, and resource materials to K–12 teachers, schools, and districts interested in developing effective service-learning programs and policies. Kinsley serves on the Board of Directors of the Corporation for National Service, and McPherson serves on the Washington Commission for National and Community Service. Both facilitate regional technical assistance centers as part of the National Service-Learning Cooperative: ServeAmerica K–12 Clearinghouse, sponsored by the National Youth Leadership Council and funded by the Corporation for National and Community Service. Kinsley also serves as a national consultant for the National Society for Experiential Education.

Contributing Authors

Caroline Allam, *Managing Director, KIDS Consortium, Portland, Maine.* Address: KIDS Consortium, c/o Southern Maine Technical College, 2 Fort Rd., South Portland, ME 04106.

Mike Bookey, *President, Digital Network Architects, Inc., Issaquah, Washington.* Address: DNA Inc., 5720 189th S.E., Issaquah, WA 98027.

Michelle Boorstein, *Reporter, Associated Press, Providence Rhode Island.* Address: Associated Press, 190 Waterman St., Providence, RI 02906.

Cory Bowman, *Assistant Director, Penn Program for Public Service, University of Pennsylvania, Philadelphia, Pennsylvania.* Address:

Center for Community Partnerships, 3440 Market St., Ste. 440, Philadelphia, PA 19104.

Mary Chamberlain, *Teacher, Rebecca Johnson School, Springfield, Massachusetts.* Address: 164 Nassau Dr., Springfield, MA 01102.

Julie Coar, *Former Student, Gig Harbor High School, Gig Harbor, Washington.* Currently a student at The Evergreen State College, 4209 Indian Pipe Loop, N.W., Bldg. U108B, Olympia, WA 98505-0003.

Sally Fellows, *Teacher, Active Citizenship Today, Omaha, Nebraska.* Address: Teachers Administrative Center, 3215 Cuming St., Omaha, NE 68131.

Ira Harkavy, *Director, Center for Community Partnerships, Assistant to the President, University of Pennsylvania, Philadelphia, Pennsylvania.* Address: Center for Community Partnerships, 3440 Market St., Ste. 440, Philadelphia, PA 19104.

Rick Jackson, *Vice President, YMCA of Greater Seattle, Seattle, Washington.* Address: YMCA of Greater Seattle, 909 Fourth Ave., Seattle, WA 98104.

Jo-Anne Wilson Keenan, *School/Family Curriculum Integration Teacher, Springfield Public Schools, Springfield, Massachusetts.* Address: 38 Edelcy Dr., Belchertown, MA 01007.

Lisa Laplante, *Project Manager, Community Service Learning Center, Springfield, Massachusetts.* Address: Community Service Learning Center, 333 Bridge St., Springfield, MA 01103.

Denise Messina, *Mediation Coordinator, Forest Park Middle School, Springfield, Massachusetts.* Address: Oakland Ave., Springfield, MA 01108.

Peter J. Negroni, *Superintendent, Springfield Public Schools, Springfield, Massachusetts.* Address: 195 State St., Springfield, MA 01103.

Janice M. Reeder, *Principal, Gig Harbor High School, Gig Harbor, Washington.* Address: Gig Harbor High School, 5101 Rosedale St., Gig Harbor, WA 98335.

Richard W. Riley, *Secretary, U.S. Department of Education, Washington, D.C.* Address: c/o Thomas G. Carroll, U.S. Department of Education, 400 Maryland Ave., S.W., Washington, DC 20202-0100.

Wokie Roberts-Weah, *Director of National Programs, National Youth Leadership Council.* Address: National Youth Leadership Council, 1910 West County Rd. B, Roseville, MN 55113.

Harry Silcox, *Director, Pennsylvania Institute for Service Learning, Philadelphia, Pennsylvania*. Address: Henry Ave. & Schoolhouse Lane, Philadelphia, PA 19144.

Len Solo, *Principal, Graham & Parks Alternative Public School, Cambridge, Massachusetts*. Address: Graham & Parks Alternative Public School, 15 Upton St., Cambridge, MA 02139. Telephone: (617) 349-6612; fax: (617) 349-6615.

James Toole and Pamela Toole, *Co-Directors, Compass Institute, St. Paul, Minnesota*. Address: Compass Institute, P.O. Box 8007, St. Paul, MN 55108. Telephone: (612) 787-0409.